NEW FORMS OF WORK

LEGAL NOTICE

Neither the European Foundation for the Improvement of Living and Working Conditions nor any person acting on behalf of the Foundation is responsible for the use which might be made of the following information.

EUROPEAN FOUNDATION FOR THE IMPROVEMENT OF LIVING AND WORKING CONDITIONS

New Forms of Work: Labour Law and Social Security Aspects in the European Community.

Original language: French

Luxembourg: Office for Official Publications of the European Communities, 1988 – 168 pp. – 160 x 235 cm

EN

ISBN: 92-825-7914-X

Catalogue number: SY-52-88-324-EN-C

Prices (excluding VAT) in Luxembourg:
ECU 12,00   BFR 500,00   IRL 9,00   UKL 8,50   USD 14,50

Printed in Ireland

NEW FORMS OF WORK

Labour Law and Social Security Aspects
in the European Community

*EUROPEAN FOUNDATION
FOR THE IMPROVEMENT OF
LIVING AND WORKING CONDITIONS*

The author: Professor Yota Kravaritou-Manitakis is Professor of Labour Law at the University of Thessaloniki, Greece. She has compiled this report for the Foundation in collaboration with a European-Community-wide group of experts in labour law and social security systems.

ACKNOWLEDGEMENTS

It has been possible to prepare this report thanks to the national reports and valuable assistance provided by the following experts: Éliane Vogel-Polsky for Belgium, Ruth Nielsen for Denmark, Gérard Lyon-Caen for France, Wolfgang Däubler for the Federal Republic of Germany, Kader Asmal for Ireland, Bruno Veneziani for Italy, Federico Dúran Lopez for Spain, Antoine Jacobs for the Netherlands, Antonio Monteiro Fernandes for Portugal, and Paul Davies for the United Kingdom.

Ms C. Dimitracos and Ms L. Mantopoulos drew up preliminary dossiers on German and French law respectively, and Ms S. Ioannidis carried out the research into Luxembourg law. The word processing of the report was done by Ms D. Zamboulis. I wish to thank them all, and also to thank the Project Manager for the trust and patience shown to me.

Yota Kravaritou-Manitakis   **Thessaloniki**
September 1987

TABLE OF CONTENTS

PROLOGUE

The revival and recognition of marginal forms of work, which have been known in the member states since the beginning of the industrial age, but which had been pushed aside both by labour law (domestic and international) and by social attitudes, are now raising a series of problems, some of which will be be dealt with in this comparative study. Its theme is the impact or the effects of "new forms of work" (also known as "atypical" or "differentiated" employment) on labour law and social security law in the member states.

The study will offer an up-to-date review of legal developments in the area of new forms of work, and proceed to a preliminary evaluation in a perspective which will not always be strictly legal. This approach is dictated by the nature and importance of the topic. Another compelling motive is the desire to divine the deeper changes running through the national industrial systems of Community countries, and discern the prospects emerging for workers' living and working conditions under new forms of employment.

The present work is divided into six parts. An introduction (I) places the new forms in context, and states the questions which have to be answered. The second chapter (II) describes the new classification and regulation of the new forms under labour law. In the third chapter (III), the effects of the development and regulation of the new forms on labour law are pointed out. The fourth part does the same with regard to social security (IV); while the fifth attempts to assess the new role of collective bargaining (V). The concluding chapter (VI) goes on to assess the development and the "treatment" of the new forms, and offers some suggestions.

PREFACE

This book is based on work sponsored by the European Foundation for the Improvement of Living and Working Conditions.

The Foundation is an autonomous Community body established by a Regulation of the Council of Ministers of the European Communities which came into force on 26th May 1987.

The Foundation was created in recognition of the fact that problems associated with improving living and working conditions were growing more numerous and complex, that Community action to resolve them should be built on scientifically-based information, and that the social partners should be associated with such action.

Aims of the Foundation

The Foundation is dedicated to assisting in the effort to improve living and working conditions of the citizens of the Member states of the European Community. This is reflected in its charter, where five areas of concern are enumerated:

- people at work
- the organisation of work and particularly job design
- problems peculiar to certain categories of workers
- long-term aspects of improvement of the environment
- the distribution of human activities in space and in time.

The subject matter of this book, Social Security and Labour Law, relates closely to two of those basic areas: man at work and problems peculiar to certain categories of workers.

The Regulation which established the Foundation directed it to work towards improving living and working conditions in the medium and long term, to take account of Community policies and to provide the Community institutions with relevant information. Suggestions on how the Foundation might achieve its aims are offered in the Regulation and include the organisation of conferences and seminars, the conclusion of research contracts, and the dissemination of information.

Changing Patterns of Work as a Research Programme of the Foundation

The Foundation's interest in this field is defined in its third four-year programme 1985-1988: ''Increasingly life at work is being dominated by the pace of change brought about by developments in new technology, their introduction and their implications. Medium and long term activities will be influenced by the latest technologies, particularly by their effects on:

- the structure of industry, private services and the public sector
- changes in work
- changes in industrial relations

Research is being undertaken to define the nature of the changes brought about by new technology, and to assess their effects on living and working conditions.''

Through its work programme, the Foundation wants to assist in the understanding of how our societies and economies manage to adjust to new forms of work organization, to changes in demand for products and services, to different forms of behaviour and continuous technological development. These issues together with the frighteningly high unemployment rates, force us to take a new look at the labour market and to redefine work. For many people, the term ''work'' has lost its original meaning of full-time gainful employment.

In 1985, the Foundation initiated research work to investigate the ways in which the labour market reacts to these changed conditions and the new forms of work which are attracting growing attention and to evaluate their social and economic implications.

The Foundation is looking at this subject from different angles in an attempt to gain a more comprehensive view of the individual factors that characterize this trend. The research done to date covers the following areas:

(a) external and internal labour markets and employment flexibility;
(b) development of job-sharing;
(c) development of telework;
(d) impact on families and social organization;
(e) psychological impact of new forms of work and activity;
(f) legal and contractual limitations to working time;
(g) work organization in co-operative undertakings;
(h) changing patterns of time use.

Some of these developments are characterised by changes in the spatial aspect of workers' living and/or working conditions, such as homework or telework. Others relate more to the temporal aspect of life inside and outside the work place. Only on the basis of a thorough knowledge of existing rules and regulations in social security and labour law can we assess the extent and direction of change which is occurring on all fronts, be it the issue of *reduction* of working time, primarily supported by the trade unions, or be it the wish to introduce greater *flexibility* in working time arrangements and work contracts, an aim primarily supported by employers and industry.

Fundamental changes are also occurring outside the formal labour market. The more difficult it is to find paid work, the more people turn to other forms of activity which do not normally have the same status, such as community work, family welfare work or "own-initiative" environmental work, to name only a few. In a society in which the type of work has for a long time determined social status, we must re-evaluate these types of activity.

The Genesis of this Book

Within the provisions of its regulation, plans for the Foundation's activities are drawn up in a series of published four-year programmes, on which annual work programmes are then based. The knowledge which the Foundation disseminates is largely self-created through sponsored research projects, the results of which are further analyzed and evaluated by the Foundation's constituent parties, i.e. both sides of industry, the governments of the Member States of the Community and the Institutions of the Community itself, primarily the Commission, the European Parliament and the Economic and Social Committee.

Within the framework of the subject matter of this book all these parties were involved in the design, implementation and evaluation of the material. To this end, two meetings were convened: in November 1986 in Brussels and in March 1987 in Dublin, where the provisional drafts of the general report were discussed. These discussions proved very rewarding and helped to get a better understanding of the issues and trends in labour law and social security, over and beyond national and political boundaries. The redrafted general report was discussed again at the seat of the Foundation in Dublin in September 1987, when representatives of the social partners, the European Community institutions, national

17

governments, the Council of Europe, the International Labour Organisation (ILO) and other experts came together for an international seminar on Evolution in Labour Law.

The positions of the various parties vis-à-vis the general thrust of this report were widely diverging. Whereas the trade union representatives found the report of enormous importance in highlighting present or future dangers for workers of falling through the social security network, if and when certain forms of flexible work would become more widespread, the employers' representatives were of the opinion that there was actually a great and unsatisfied demand for ''less protected'' work forms, particularly where social security coverage was secured through another member in the same family. In this respect, the employers' group found the tenor of the report unnecessarily alarming and pessimistic. Following from this necessarily controversial, yet rational and fruitful, discussion of the subject matter at the international seminar, the demands for action ranged from ''no need for action'' all the way to calls for the creation of a new body of labour protection legislation at European level in order to safeguard the human and social rights of ''atypical'' workers.

The subject matter as such is basically factual and non-controversial. Nonetheless, the underlying political interests make this subject matter highly sensitive. If this volume could contribute to a rational approach to the discussion of future developments in social security protection of ''new'' or ''atypical'' work forms, the Foundation's and the individual contributors' intentions and efforts would be more than fully rewarded. The judgement on the validity of the arguments advanced in this book must be left to the reader. The researchers involved in this project accept their responsibility for these arguments. They would welcome comment and constructive critique.

Eberhard Köhler
Research Manager
European Foundation for the
Improvement of Living and Working Conditions

I
INTRODUCTION:
NEW FORMS OF WORK

SOME FEATURES OF THE NEW FORMS OF WORK

The new forms of work involve an atypical employment relationship, where the job is not of indefinite duration or full-time; or it is not carried on in the company premises; or it suggests the existence of two employers, or even the absence of any employer. We have, in short, an employment relationship which does not bring together the features of the classical subordinate work relationship as found in the typical employment contract, which a short time ago was still seen as the almost exclusive model, and was in any case the dominant one.

The new forms of work first appeared in practice slightly more than ten years ago. The innovation which they introduced did not consist in the actual content. Fixed-term employment, part-time working, home-based work, and temporary employment already existed in some countries. Labour law had taken an interest in the area up to a point, by authorising these kinds of work under certain conditions, while considering them as marginal forms of employment. What is new about them now is mainly: (a) their "irresistible", unprecedented spread in all member States, with or without an employment contract: self-employment, or employment in the black economy; (b) their recognition by certain legal systems, not always without some hesitation, using regulations which are not consistent with the principles governing labour law, so that it has some difficulty in accommodating them; (c) the fact that as they are encouraged — and promoted — by both governments and employers, the trade union organisations (currently in a weakened condition) have no option but to accept them,[1] despite the reservations and even the hostility

---

1. Unemployment and job losses in industry have weakened the trade union movement. This weakening has coincided with a strengthening in the position of the employers who, condemning the inflexibility of labour legislation and the excessive burdens which it imposes, have been trying to obtain changes in the law on security of employment, to cut costs in order to deal with the crisis, and to get more flexibility in recruitment procedures. The fact that certain governments have been receptive to these arguments

19

which some people have expressed about these changes on account of their negative repercussions on — among other things — collective rights and trade union action in general. In fact, there is a direct link between some degree of paralysis in union action and the development of these new forms of work, which have burst upon the scene without giving any opportunity to work out a long-term policy.

For a long time it was thought that this was a passing phenomenon connected with the economic crisis. The structural nature of the changes is, however, well-known to everyone by now.

The typical employment relationship, by comparison with the "discreet charm" of the new varieties (as perceived by companies), is losing ground. Thus, the new forms stand in total contrast to the traditional work relationship. One finds a new type of distinction, between employment contracts, for which most textbooks on labour law, and most authors dealing with employment contracts, make no allowance. In the classic distinctions drawn between employment contracts[2] in labour law, one finds special rules which govern work done by women, by children or by handicapped people. Now, employment contracts designed for special categories of worker, while following the guidelines of the typical contract, strengthen the protection which it offers. A distinction is also drawn between the classic employment contract and the sectoral rules governing marine work, transport work, etc. Now these rules, dealing with some specific aspects of sectoral employment, do not seek to derogate from the principles which govern the typical employment relationship. On the other hand, what the new forms of employment do is to introduce procedures which derogate from those principles, from the legislation which protects workers. According to one author with experience of a comparative nature: "Atypical employment relationships are something more important, more far-reaching, which affects the very foundations of productive activity. In a certain sense, one may see them as an alarm signal or as the sign of the change in attitude in contrast with the traditional employment contract. They indicate that the foundations of labour law are being called into question, that is

partly explains the progress made by various forms of "atypical" employment. See Efren Cordova, "Les relations d'emploi atypiques: leur importance et leurs répercussions" (based on the summary report of the national reports on "atypical employment relationships", the second point on the agenda at the 11th Conference of the International Society for Labour Law and Social Security, held in Caracas in September 1985, BIS, 1986.

2. See for example the distinctions drawn by H. Barbagelata in his chapter entitled "Different categories of workers" in *Comparative Labour Law and Industrial Relations* (edited by R. Blanpain), Kluver 1982, pp. 320 ff.

to say, the socio-economic base which has provided the model for the preparation of employment regulations."[3]

It should be pointed out that there is no single text, either an agreement or a recommendation, from the International Labour Organisation (ILO) which deals with the new forms of work in their current context: they have always been seen as exceptional forms of employment relationship, to be avoided if possible.[4] There is, admittedly, the international labour agreement no. 96 on employment agencies, which has been ratified by the majority of member States, but its objective is to control employment contracts according to the established logic.[5] On the other hand, at community level, where misgivings have been voiced several times as to the development of new forms of work, there are many legal texts dealing with this problem. Mostly, these texts are plans for directives. The most important one is the modified text of the proposal for a directive on *temporary work and fixed-term employment contracts*[6] of 1984. This was drawn up following a European Parliament resolution in 1981, dealing with the development of temporary employment. The need was "to forestall abuses in this area". The objectives of the draft directive are:

a) to protect temporary employees by giving them the rights of permanent workers;

b) to protect permanent jobs against an improper use of temporary employment (which is less expensive for the employer);

c) to guarantee the standards and quality of temporary employment companies against abuses;

d) to protect workers employed under fixed-term contracts by applying the collective agreements of permanent employees, the written form of the contract, etc..

The draft also calls for worker representatives to be informed on

---

3. E. Cordova, "Les relations d'emploi atypiques," loc. cit., p. 16. In a more recent article, the author emphasises that this is "a phenomenon without precedent in the history of labour law". See "De l'emploi total au travail atypique: vers un virage dans l'évolution des relations de travail," *Revue Internationale du Travail*, November- December 1986, p. 715.

4. See N. Valticos, *Droit international de travail*, Dalloz, Paris.

5. This convention has been ratified by Belgium only as regards its second part. In France, where it has been ratified in its entirety, it is considered that it is not applicable to temporary employment companies.

6. See the initial draft of the directive in Official Journal C128, 1982, and the modified proposal in Official Journal C133, 21.5.1986.

the number of atypical workers. The typical employment relationship remains the rule.

Another proposal for a directive deals with *part-time working.*[7] The aim is not to create special regulations, but to extend to part-time employees the rules which apply to full-time employees, in order to avoid discrimination and secure the observance of the principle of proportional rights.

The existence of these proposals for directives is also a sign of the importance which now attaches to the new forms of employment, and the preoccupations that these have aroused in the Community.

THE SCALE AND IMPENETRABILITY OF THE NEW FORMS

In Europe at present, illusion still holds out at times.
For a few seconds, I seem to recognise a light breeze.

Henri Michaux, *Au pays de la Magie*

The scale of these developments is extensive in all member states. The first impression was that the development of new forms of employment varied from one Community country to the next; that it was especially some "central" countries which had seen this extraordinary growth: the United Kingdom, France, the Federal Republic of Germany, Italy, Belgium. It was thought that it was less marked in countries such as Spain, Greece, Portugal, Denmark or Ireland. Now, in fact, as the present research project has revealed, there is no member state in which the signs of the new forms of work are merely growing or staying at a discreet level. What does vary is the level of awareness of the scale of atypical employment. Another thing which varies from state to state is the legal "treatment" of atypical work, as will be seen in what follows.

Even before they had been identified and named as "new forms of work" — or "atypical work" or "differentiated work" — and before being seen as a legal phenomenon tending to have their own logic and features, these forms of work, maintaining uneasy relations with labour law and social security law, were already quite widespread, especially in southern countries: Italy, Spain, Greece and Portugal. The "swelling" in atypical work has not yet troubled the competent agencies — the government and the social partners — in countries

---

7. See Official Journal C52, 12.3.1982, and Official Journal C18, 22.1.1983 for the modified text.

such as Ireland, Greece, Portugal and even Denmark. In Denmark, employment conditions have perhaps not deteriorated very far as yet, while the thick network of collective negotiations and the social security system help to absorb the negative effects of the new forms of work. The situation is different in France, Italy, the Federal Republic of Germany, Belgium and even Spain. In those countries, there was a quicker growth in awareness of the extent of the specific problems posed by atypical employment. This growth of awareness is also affected by the features of the industrial relations system, the labour market, and the state of the trade union movement and government policies.

We do not have enough data to make a precise and convincing assessment of the penetration of new forms of work. Statistics are not arranged in such a way, it would seem, as to provide even a rough picture — let alone an exact one — of atypical employment in general. In any case certain new forms of work, those of which the law is unaware, are by definition hard to grasp. In fact the law, in so far as it acts to regulate the new forms which spring into being incessantly, can only deal with a portion of the atypical employment relationships, not including the ones which flourish in the underground world of the black economy. Thus, despite the more or less systematic or repeated intervention of legislators in certain countries, such as France or the Federal Republic of Germany, there are new forms which lie outside the framework of law; there are also some which are quite simply illegal. There is a widespread feeling that every time the law manages to regulate an employment relationship, another atypical employment relationship immediately comes into being, frustrating the restraints envisaged by the regulations and thus maintaining the condition of obscurity in which they currently exist.

A typical example of obscurity in atypical employment may be found in the case of Greece.[8] It has not been possible to find studies or investigations on atypical employment, and it has not yet been subjected to legal reform. The first response on part-time working or temporary working, for example, would be that these forms of employment are almost non-existent: part-time workers stand at the lowest rate of all member states (2.1%);[9] temporary employment companies are prohibited. But the structure of the labour market

---

8. See Constantin Tsoukalas, "Classes unidimensionnelles et sujets 'polyvalents'", *Revue Anti*, 1984, 267; and by the same author, "Sujets polyvalents et relations des classes dans le capitalisme contemporain", *Revue des Sciences Sociales*, Athens, 1985, number 56, pp. 3 ff.

9. See OECD, *Employment Outlook*, September 1983, pp. 44 and 50.

would suggest a certain degree of caution. The proportion of self-employed is very high, for a start — the highest of any member state — while the proportion of salaried employees does not exceed 48% of the active population. It is known that a very high number of workers have two different activities, one of which is usually not declared — an unofficial part-time job. If official data show a large percentage of the active population without jobs, this is partly due to the non-transparency of activities in the black economy. But those obscure activities which elude the statistics, which are multifunctional and alternative activities, in fact take place on a major scale: atypical employment is widespread in Greece. The question arises in similar terms in Portugal. In each country, in any case, atypical work throws up a dominant new format of employment, which may be with or without a contract.

THE HUNDRED FACES OF THE NEW FORMS OF WORK

The number of varieties which new forms of work can show is striking; and it seems that the profusion of forms is growing day by day. There are certainly well-known forms of atypical employment, which are tending to emerge from their centuries-old marginal position: fixed-term working, temporary working, part-time working, home-based working. These well-known forms, however, are currently presenting many hitherto unknown versions. Thus, part-time working is producing job-sharing, job-splitting, office-sharing, vertical part-time working and horizontal part-time working. Under the heading of fixed-term contracts, allowance has to be made for youth training contracts in countries such as Italy, Belgium and Germany. In other countries, such as England and Ireland, a training contract is not an employment contract. One may find, in a single country, several different new forms of work involving young people: some of these forms are less concerned with an effective training programme than with providing extremely short-term jobs, lasting for six weeks or three months. They are thus different from the traditional forms of apprenticeship contract. This category of contracts dealing with work experience programmes, training and apprenticeship is currently undergoing massive expansion in all countries, and is often the subject of new legal regulations.

There are also certain new forms of employment contracts which have never been seen before, such as labour on call, the German "KAPOVAZ", intermittent working and alternating working. One may also mention solidarity contracts in Italy, which are collective company agreements which have an impact on the individual contract. Now, the new typology of employment contracts, which varies from country to country and which sometimes includes illegal forms of contract, certainly fails to account for the range of new forms practised by workers who present themselves under the heading of self-employed. This is often the case with home-based workers and their most modern variant: home-based teleworkers. It is often the case, too, with subcontracting, a phenomenon which is gaining ground at a rapid pace, especially in countries where there is a prohibition against firms using temporary employment. In order to see this many-faceted phenomenon to its full extent, one must add the forms of atypical work in the informal part of the economy: "black" or "grey" employment which is often disguised as self-employment, and clandestine employment which leaves no trace at all.

In order to complete the list of new forms — which is really inexhaustible — and in order to show the "crumbling" effect which is currently affecting employment, one should also add the category of jobs without security which have been created through programmes of employment for the unemployed, who are taken on particularly by local authorities and the social services. In France one finds the "TUC" programme (*travaux d'utilité collective*: public utility work), in Belgium the "CST" (*cadre spécial temporaire*: special temporary staff), while similar categories exist in Denmark, the Netherlands, the Federal Republic of Germany, Britain and Spain with the temporary social co-operation work programme. These are contracts with a limited duration — a very limited duration — which receive subventions from the state, which covers more than half the wage costs: the aim is to ease the cost of unemployment payments (a worker employed under these schemes often costs less than an unemployed person). These atypical forms of work are precarious and vulnerable.

Another form of working which is also reappearing and spreading is unpaid voluntary work.

While this "atypical employment" phenomenon can find a huge variety of practical formulations, it chooses a different kind of expression in each country, through a particular form which is predominant. This may be with or without an employment contract. In Portugal, it is the fixed-term contract; Spain is the same; Greece is largely similar, although home-based working (contracted work) is very widespread; in Denmark and the Federal Republic of Germany the predominant form seems to be part-time working, which is also true of the United Kingdom (although this country has the most complete range of practices); while in Belgium it is temporary working.

25

In countries which ban the "marketing" of labour, the favourite practices are subcontracting and "lending" workers. Italy is the undisputed champion of home-grown clandestine employment, but foreign immigrants are known to work in the black economies of Germany, Belgium and France. In Italy too, but also in Belgium, contracts of employment and apprenticeship are flourishing within the new regulatory framework. This gives a picture (though not an exhaustive one) of the "endless" list of the forms of work which set out to distinguish and distance themselves from the classical employment contract, once the only "star" in the firmament of labour law.

THE GENDER OF THE NEW FORMS

The majority of workers employed under a new form of work, or at least under a contract of the new type, are women.[10] Studies and investigations, particularly into part-time contracts, have shown that in all member states the overwhelming majority of workers in this category are female. The proportion is higher than 70%, and sometimes reaches 90%. The same is true of temporary working, and home-based working. The explanation is obvious: the double rôle of women in our society obliges them to work at jobs which allow them to meet their domestic commitments — to look after the children and do the household chores.

After women, the next highest categories of workers in atypical employment are young people (apprentices, work experience participants, students), foreigners, elderly workers, and the unemployed. Most of these atypical employees belong, in other words, to the new social groupings, sometimes called "new minorities", which have appeared in massive numbers on the labour market, and which at the same time maintain a different view of life and work. Now, one finds that more and more frequently male workers are in atypical employment positions, under pressure from the economic crisis and the employment policies of member states. Despite this, male workers still remain in the minority for the time being. The feminisation of many new forms of work may also serve to underline the existence of another myth which is seen as a feature of the traditional employment contract: the notion that work is

10. See, inter alia, Jean-Pierre Jallade, "Mythes et réalités d'une politique du temps partiel", in *Pour une nouvelle politique sociale en Europe* (directed by J. Vandamme; preface by J. Delors), Economica, Paris, 1984, p. 112.

masculine by gender.[11] This does not appear to be the case with quite a considerable number of new forms of employment.

LEGAL REGULATIONS VARY FROM ONE COUNTRY TO ANOTHER

While neither the scale of the new forms, nor the awareness of them, appears in the same way from one country to another, another factor which varies is the legal "treatment" of these phenomena. This is true particularly in the sense that there are countries which seem to slide around the specific legal problems posed by the new forms of work, and have not yet proceeded to carry out reforms in this area. This is the case notably in Denmark, Greece, Portugal and the Grand Duchy of Luxembourg, but also in the Netherlands and to a certain extent in the United Kingdom and Ireland. On the other hand France, Italy, the Federal Republic of Germany, Spain and Belgium have already made changes in their legislation and proceeded to regulate atypical employment. The legal means adopted for this process of "adapting" the law to new forms of working are not, as we shall see, the same in all countries, nor is there a complete coincidence in the extent of the reforms introduced.

THE DICHOTOMY: HARD-CORE WORKERS AND PERIPHERAL WORKERS

The major consequence of the new forms of work and the new typology of employment contracts, whether or not they have been subject to a special process of reform, is a split in the salary-earning staff. On one side there are the workers who have a typical employment relationship: full-time, with an open-ended contract and so forth. They enjoy the protection laid down in labour law and the rights conferred by the social security system. These employees are seen as belonging to the hard core which is indispensable to the running of the company. And on the other side there are the "peripheral" workers, who have an atypical employment relationship and a lower status. They get lower pay, reduced or non-existent protection against dismissal, and similarly reduced or non-existent

---

11. See *Le sexe du travail* (various authors), Paris, 1984.

benefits. From a legal point of view, this dichotomy corresponds —
in certain countries such as France, following the new law of 1986
— to the distinction drawn between jobs and tasks, which is
appropriate in the case of peripheral workers.

Workers who work outside the company, but who are effectively
related to it, also have a lower type of status. Their existence may
be attributed to the explosion of the large firm and the consequent
erosion of the community, or else to an employment policy, pursued
by the firm, in favour of this "lightening of the burden". In the sub-
category of workers outside the firm, one often finds several groups
which are not clearly identified. The result is in any case a
multiplication of statuses: the traditional employee status, the various
"new types" of status for those working within the company, and
the different status (which may vary according to circumstances) of
those who work outside the firm but whose work is for the firm. One
can already see the consequences of this diversity in the status of
workers — who are divided into various categories and sub-categories
— when it comes to exercising their collective rights.[12]

THE QUESTION IS NOT "FLEXIBILITY", BUT LACK OF SECURITY

The term "flexibility" is often used to refer to the essential substance
and content of the new forms of work. This term is neither accurate
nor particularly apt.[13] Although there are connections with the
reduction and rationalisation of working time, the basic questions
raised by the new forms of employment are:

   a) the growth in impermanent employment, which has created
      different problems in the adaptability of working time: a flexible
      timetable in the framework of a typical employment contract
      might have been desirable from the point of view of the workers
      themselves, under certain circumstances. The new forms of
      work offer the prospect of a whole working life with periods

---

12. On the problems raised by "a dual division of society with on the one hand an élite
    group of employees, and on the other hand a mass of unemployed and half-employed
    people taken up with little jobs", and how trade unions, among others, are facing
    this situation, see the debate between Peter Glotz, Tilman Fichter and André Gorz:
    "La plus grande liberté possible. Emancipation dans le travail et émancipation du
    travail." *Temps Modernes*, October 1986, pp. 65 ff.

13. On the "fleeting" and precarious nature of the new forms of work, see Emilio
    Valenzuela, "Formas atipicas de trabajo y las relaciones laboriales", Caracas conference
    report, vol.II pp. 117 ff., p. 189.

of inactivity, or a career made up of "little jobs", meaning several parallel jobs or tasks which do not guarantee any continuity or stability.

b) the fact that the new forms of work remove from salaried employees with an atypical contract that protection provided by the labour law of member states, while preventing them from satisfying the conditions required to qualify for the rights and benefits conferred by the social security system.[14] One cannot confuse the adaptability of working time and its problems[15] — at least its theoretical problems — with the wider problems of new forms of employment.

One of the five main definitions of flexibility in relation to its objectives, in Boyer's study of flexibility at work in Europe, concerns us here. This is where flexibility comes up against the weakness of the legal constraints governing the employment contract, and in particular governing decisions on dismissal.[16] The shifting concept of flexibility has been used, according to the European unions, to "wipe out a good proportion of the social advances which have been obtained during the last forty years in Western Europe".[17] At the same time, according to the group of experts presided over by Ralf Dahrendorf, flexibility is not a panacea for all the ills of society and the economy. It is one resource, and not the most important one. Employment protection and the protection of the various types of employment contract is in any case only one of the factors on which flexibility in the labour market depends. Moreover, security of employment is a legitimate demand.[18] In other words, flexibility cannot be a positive development if it reduces (or abolishes) the protection of job security, but only if it takes its place within a general context of dynamism and innovation at all levels of economic and political decision-making.[19] So far, as we shall see, the new forms

---

14. One of the problems to be studied is the intensity of working (for example, in teleworking) and the repercussions of this on the timetable.

15. See European Foundation for the Improvement of Living and Working Conditions - R. Blanpain, *Legal and contractual limitations to working time in the member countries of the European Community* (Summary Report), 1986.

16. See Boyer (ed), *La flexibilité du travail en Europe*, Editions La Découverte, Paris, 1986, pp. 237 ff.

17. Institut syndical européen, *Flexibilités et emplois - mythes et réalités*, pp. 2 and 4.

18. See OECD, *La flexibilité du marché du travail* (report of a group of high-level experts to the Secretary General), Paris, 1986.

19. This is also the thrust of Guy Standing's remarks. He believes that "it is at least surprising that at the moment when, in Western Europe, we are experiencing

of work have harmed security of employment and undermined the rights won by workers.

FORMS OF WORK ARE CHANGING IN LINE WITH COMPANY INTERESTS

Changing forms of work are certainly not alien either to the new economic organisation which has arisen over the past fifteen years (notably through the multinationalisation of capital which has encouraged employment transfers on a global basis) or to the procedures which commercial law has given to big companies to facilitate the decentralisation of management: setting up subsidiaries, taking over control, subcontracting.[20] The labour market has felt the effects of the new organisation through the employment problems which have arisen, and also by the new forms of employment overtaking traditional forms. This simply shows the new personnel policies being pursued by companies. Whereas for a long time companies had an interest in greater stability in employment, and needed a permanent supply of trained staff, this is nowadays not always quite the position. The new logic dictates that "the workforce must never be in a non-productive state, and can be laid off when there is a falling-off in orders."[21] Likewise, in big stores, when there are no customers neither will there be any idle sales staff.

Paid time must corespond to actual working time — and this principle is based on the principle of non-permanent employment, even if the name given to it is "flexibility". Businesses only want to take on commitments in strict proportion to their immediate needs. The new forms of work have arisen under the pressure of these demands of companies; labour law has changed, or rather has had change forced on it, in this context.

---

simultaneously increased job flexibility and rising unemployment, some authors are attributing these unemployment rates to lack of flexibility in the workforce. It is equally surprising that a number of rights won by workers during the lengthy period of full employment are now being blamed as elements of inflexibility responsible for the outbreak of that apparently virulent disease that has been dubbed, by common consent, 'Eurosclerosis' ''.

20. Pointed out by G. Lyon-Caen as early as 1980. See "Plasticité du capital et nouvelles formes d'emploi", *Droit Social*, September-October 1980, pp. 8 ff.

21. Ibid.

THE CONFUSION CAUSED FOR LABOUR AND SOCIAL SECURITY LAW

It is characteristic of the new forms, or more precisely of the different types of contracts which are now proliferating, that they derogate from the rules of the classic employment contract on which the labour law of Community countries is based. It can also happen that individual labour contracts or even company agreements derogate from some general principles of labour law. Worse still: in some countries, new regulations, imposed by law, which relate to new forms of work and activity are distancing themselves from the spirit of the law to reintroduce, sometimes under new-sounding names, old forms of employment and practices which were rejected in the nineteenth century when labour law was almost non-existent. If that is the case for forms of employment which come under the new variants of employment contracts, there are other forms of employment which lie entirely outside the law: the new category of self-employed known in Italy as "para-subordinates", as well as those working in the black economy who elude the rules of labour law not partially — as with the new types of employment contract — but totally. Thus there has developed a kind of law which Professor G. Lyon-Caen calls simply "activity law", parallel to labour law; and real labour law is losing ground to the new arrival. Activity law is an expression, among other things, of a sort of return to self-employment, with the proviso, however, that this time the supposedly independent workers involved are not really self-employed at all.

As far as the law on new forms of work is concerned, there are other consequences: the suppression of protection for workers, the abandonment of rights which have been won, discrimination between workers, non-recognition of the principle of equality, etc. The development of new forms thus strikes at the very heart of labour law in member states, at its raison d'être as regards one of its vital functions, concerned with protecting the workers rather than the company. In effect, labour law in Community countries — the situation is different in some ways in the US and Japan — is a law based on public policy, progressively built up in order to guarantee that all workers have a minimum level of protection. Social security law has a parallel objective: it provides minimum protection to workers exposed to social hazards: redundancy, accidents, illness, etc. The

---

22. This is the case, for example, in the United Kingdom. See Lord Wedderburn, "The new industrial relations laws in Great Britain", *Labour and Society*, vol. 10, January 1985, pp. 45 ff. (especially p. 58).

new forms of work, by following the other parallel path — which in some countries is embodied in legislation[22] — represents such a threat to labour law that in certain countries one might well ask why the Labour Code should not simply be "thrown in the fire"[23], and whether we have finally reached the era of "the end of labour law".[24]

In this research report, an attempt will be made to define the current relationship between instances of atypical employment and labour law. Is it a case of "labour law versus the new forms of work", in a sort of duel?[25] Could the flexible, varied and imaginative new forms of work "fertilise" the field of labour law, making it adapt to the present-day need for new solutions? Or will they remove all vestiges of social protection and leave the salaried employee — at least the atypical worker — naked and unprotected once again as he was at the beginning of the industrial age?[26] There will also be a "re-evaluation" of the principle of contractual independence which brings the company (the employer) face to face with the worker, unaccompanied by any union representatives, to sign his or her individual employment contract — described by Kahn-Freund as "a fig-leaf to hide the worker's substantially subordinate position".[27] What prospects for the future do the new forms of work offer to the two branches of law which have been overwhelmed, which concern themselves with the minimum protection of wage-earners under a capitalist system, and which have also been shaped by their own struggles over the centuries?

One might perhaps wonder, too, whether the appearance of the new forms of work, which can be dated to about 1974 — at the same time as the oil crisis, the realisation of the impact of multinationals on industrial relations, the introduction of new technology, mass unemployment — marks the beginning of a new era for labour law in the Community's member states.

---

23. See the article in *Intersocial* number 113 (May 1985) entitled "Faut-il brûler le Code du travail?", pp. 8-10, and under the same title, the proceedings of the Montpellier colloquium (25 April 1986), *Droit Social*, pp. 559 ff.

24. B. Boubli, "A propos de la flexibilité d'emploi: vers la fin du droit du travail?", *Droit Social*, April 1985, p. 239-240.

25. See Raymond Soubi,"Après les négociations sur la flexibilité", *Droit Social*, April 1985, pp. 201 ff.

26. See "Les changements des structures économiques en Europe et leurs effets sur les relations professionnelles", *Travail et Société*, 1985, pp. 82 ff.; and R. Blanpain, "Ajustements structurels et relations professionnelles: aspects de droit du travail", *Travail et Société*, 1985, pp. 197 ff.

27. See the discussion at the 3rd Pontignano international seminar, ibid., p. 266.

NEW FORMS OF WORK: THE FUTURE BEFORE THEM

We are realising more and more that the new forms of work, by virtue of their acceptance — by legislators, by collective agreements, by lawyers, or by the so-called informal sector of the economy, depending on which country is involved — no longer look like transitory forms of employment, imposed for the moment by the economic crisis. While they are sought first of all by companies (or rather, by employers), they are at the same time encouraged by the governments of all countries. The public authorities believe, in fact, that the atypical forms are a useful weapon in the fight against unemployment, and have adopted a policy of actively promoting the new kinds of work. The trade union organisations, despite their opposition to these developments as a general rule, and despite their attachment to the guarantees offered to workers by the traditional employment relationship, cannot turn back the tide. The unions can only acquiesce in the introduction of new forms of work, especially when they are sanctioned and regulated at company level. At times, indeed, the new forms — on those rare occasions when they are freely chosen — may express a new social attitude to work, a desire to give more importance to living time (time for personal or family concerns, or for unpaid creative activities) rather than working time. The same is true of the attitude shown by some young fathers who decide to cut down their working time in order to share the upbringing of their children.

The fact is that "the law has been left behind"[28] — in the sense that the law has not taken a systematic and comprehensive approach to new forms of work, and notably to recent developments in employment contracts, which follow a new logic going against the principles of the typical contract. The novelty of the phenomenon, and its scale, have certainly proved surprising, and not just to the trade union organisations. It still remains to set up a common vocabulary at Community level to cover all the variants and the overall problems which the new developments have thrown up for labour law and social security in member states. The novelty of the phenomenon may also be seen from the fact that in some countries, such as Portugal, Greece or Denmark, the handbooks of labour law devote little attention and even less space to atypical employment.

It also seems that the new forms of work are partly explicable in terms of the present transitional phase in the process of reorganisation

---

28. W. Wedderburn, *Workers and the Law*, 3rd edition, London, 1986, p. 117.

of capital, which is moving through a "meta-Fordist" phase, and by its revaluation at national and Community (international) level.[29] In this context — of the reorganisation of capital, but also of new social attitudes to working — the new forms of employment and activity may well herald the organisation of work in the next century.

If that is the case, the law ought to take a long-term view of these developments.

QUESTIONS TO WHICH AN ANSWER WILL BE SOUGHT

The main aim of the present research project is to reveal the effects of the development of new forms of employment and activity (otherwise known as differentiated working or atypical employment) on labour law and social security law in the member states.

To achieve this objective, the first step will not be to present an overview of new forms, but rather to discuss the legal regulation of the most significant forms. The most characteristic cases and the most important regulations will be cited in order to illustrate the trends in the law in these areas, without being exhaustive at all times on the full range of countries — which in any case would be impossible, as one does not find the same forms everywhere. This study in comparative law will naturally deal with legal regulations currently in force, as the new forms of work have no legal antecedents which would affect the primary concern here.

Throughout this report, reference will be made to data which are not strictly legal, to figures and to special features of the various countries under discussion, bearing in mind that "the use of comparative law for practical purposes becomes an abuse only if it is informed by a legalist spirit which ignores the context of the law".[30]

An attempt will then be made to assess the impact of the new forms of work on the labour law of member states. Has the law been

---

29. The current phase of capitalist development is seeing a shift from "Fordism" to "meta-Fordism"; this term expresses not only a model of work organisation but also a model of capital accumulation, which appeared in 1913 and also includes the forms of new technology in the 1970s. On this question see, among others, Boyer (ed.), *La flexibilité du travail en Europe*, loc. cit.

30. As pointed out by a major theorist of labour law and comparative law, Otto Kahn-Freund: "On Uses and Misuses of Comparative Law", *The Modern Law Review*, 1974, p. 27.

distorted by the development of new forms? Do these forms lie outside the reach of its protective measures? What happens to workers' individual rights, and also to their collective rights, under the new forms of work? The question will also arise as to whether a two-tier labour law is emerging, or rather, there will be a discussion of the extent of the overtaking of labour law by "activity law".

Is the law of social security in member states taking account of the workers under new forms of employment, and how far does this go? Is adequate coverage being provided for the new social hazards facing the atypical workers, or is the traditional employment relationship still always taken as the standard of reference? If that is not the case, what benefits are available to those atypical workers, and what are their specific problems to be resolved?

In examining the effectiveness of the legal methods and techniques used to adapt traditional labour law to the new requirements of the economy, an attempt will also be made to bring out the rôle of the trade union organisations in this process of adaptation.

The concluding section will attempt to provide an answer, as far as this is possible, to the general question which F. Piotet and E. Köhler raised at the Brussels colloquium, as to how appropriate existing measures are to the new forms of work, and how they could be made to work in a positive way.

In the knowledge, finally, that "economic development is not an end in itself, but a means of attaining a social objective, namely a better life for all, and especially for the disadvantaged,"[31] particular attention will be paid, among the solutions worked out in member countries to deal with new forms of work and the proposals advanced, to those solutions which respect the nature of European labour law as it has been shaped over many years. This law, while serving the market economy of the member countries, has taken care — under the watchful eye of the workers and the trade union organisations — to provide a minimum degree of protection to people working in a subordinate position.

---

31. See the introduction by the Director of the ILO, in *Rapport sur l'évolution du monde du travail*, Geneva, 1985. See also the statement by Oliver Clark in "La flexibilité du marché du travail: les deux faces du phénomène", *BIS*, 3/4 1985, p. 40: "It would certainly be wrong to draw the conclusion ... that we must proceed to a radical revision of the social measures adopted in recent decades, even though the progress achieved in this way has led to regrettable inflexibilities in the workings of the labour market. What should instead be done, as objectively as possible, is to try to analyse each case where lack of flexibility seems to be undermining the effectiveness of the workforce, bearing in mind both the social value and the economic cost."

II
NEW FORMS OF WORK
WITH OR WITHOUT
EMPLOYMENT CONTRACTS

AN ATTEMPT AT CLASSIFICATION: TOWARDS A NEW TYPOLOGY OF EMPLOYMENT CONTRACTS

> There are seven kinds of fog (I am referring to the principal kinds) and the third of these is enough to prevent you from seeing your own horse as you climb onto it.
>
> H. Michaux, *Au pays de la Magie*

Under the general heading of new forms of work we find a complete range of jobs, starting with part-time working, which at times, under certain conditions, is not too far removed from traditional, or "typical", forms of employment. Then we have fixed-term employment, temporary employment, home-based working, self-employment, small jobs, and finally, at the other end of the scale, black-market employment. Here we may consider merely some of the best-known practices in the area which concerns us, the "dim haze" which, according to economists, covers the transition between employment and unemployment. The different new forms which we find in this position can give the impression of forming a continuous chain: as the chain moves further on, there is a steady decrease in the protection which labour law has provided for traditional employment, until at the end of the scale — as for example in the case of black-market employment — this protection disappears completely.

Now, since a common feature of the new forms of work is that they exclude people recruited in this way from the protection of general labour legislation, one might conclude, on closer inspection, that all of these new forms of work can be designated by a comprehensive term such as atypical employment or abnormal employment (in Italy they also use the term abnormal forms of work). This would, however, be incorrect because, first of all, there are very significant differences between the new forms of work themselves. For example, there are few shared features between part-time working and fake self-employment. Also, it would be inappropriate to confer an inferior status on the new forms of employment.

The term "atypical work" has however been used to refer to the phenomenon (at the Caracas conference), and this continues at the present time — for reasons of convenience, obviously, but also because it is not always easy to classify the new forms of work. The concepts have not yet been fully worked out, even in the member countries where attention has been paid to them by legislators, case law and legal literature. In spite of everything, we will attempt a classification. This is merely a suggestion, and needs to be elaborated more fully.

In drawing an overall distinction between the new forms of work and traditional employment, the contrast brings out (with a small number of exceptions) the essential feature of the new forms, which is their insecurity. Now, the idea of insecurity suggests precisely the notion of a "short job". In cases such as this, "task would be a better term than job".[1] This term denotes "employment" for a limited time, for a limited function, for a limited duration; therefore we are dealing with an insecure job "by definition". What workers have to do under the new forms of employment is to carry out tasks in a condition of greater or lesser subordination, and perhaps also in a state of semi-independence. The distinction proposed would bring out the two basic legal models of employment, which can correspond to two sets of rules, applying to traditional employment and new forms of work respectively. Although it does exist in French law, and although it has been confirmed in recent legislation in the area, the distinction between job and task has not been developed in the other member states where, however, the new forms continue to point up the difference between "brief jobs" and "traditional employment".

Within the category of new forms of work, there is a major distinction which needs to be drawn straight away. On the one hand there are new forms which come under an employment contract — the various contractual variants, as Cordova[2] puts it: the fixed-term contract, the temporary work contract, the part-time work contract — and on the other hand there are new forms with no contract; one can put self-employed work under this heading, of course, but fake subcontracting and grey- and black-market work also belong here.

If insecurity, or rather the time element and the duration of

---

1. G. Lyon-Caen, "Plasticité du capital et nouvelles formes d'emploi", loc. cit. p. 9.

2. "De l'emploi total au travail atypique: vers un virage dans l'évolution des relations du travail", loc. cit. p. 718.

employment contracts, is the first criterion in distinguishing new forms of employment contracts from the traditional sort, another criterion which has been pointed out is that of a multiplicity of employers.[3] In the classic contract, there is one employer, but in many new-style contracts there are several: the employment relationship is a triangular one in temporary employment contracts, in subcontracting, and in transfers of personnel. This category of contracts for new forms would appear to be one manifestation of the tendency for employment to move outside the company structure.

Another criterion for distinguishing new-style contracts could perhaps be the involvement of the public authorities — or even incentives from them — in concluding the contract (under the guise of financial intervention: social or fiscal concessions). This criterion would serve, for example, to distinguish between the typical employment contract and such contracts as job-training schemes for young people, as well as contracts made with long-standing job applicants. In this category of contract, one notes the presence of a third party, along with the usual two contracting parties (the employer and the employee).

If one wishes to come back to the basic classification underlying the new forms of work, between the new range of contracts on the one hand, and uncontracted work (self-employed and black-market) on the other hand, mention should also be made of home-based working and teleworking. In these two cases, the criterion of subordination which marks the previous distinction is not always clearcut and highly visible. Just as, in the area of "new" self-employed working, the traditional criterion of subordination slips between the fingers and becomes invisible, similarly in the case of home-based working and teleworking, it can be there and then disappear from view: the worker who was in the condition of an employee becomes self-employed. But he or she transfers to the legal status of self-employed without thereby moving away from the position of economic dependence in which his or her work was done up to then.

If one follows the theory that there is not just one normal type of employment, summed up in the classic employment contract (though this is not so clear in all member countries), but rather that there are two major types — the other type being the one realised through the new forms — then one may proceed to identify, within this second major type, the two axes around which the new forms develop. One of them gives us what G. Lyon-Caen[4] has called the job with no

---

3. See Jean Pelissier, "La relation atypique du travail", loc. cit.

4. "Plasticité du capital et nouvelles formes", loc. cit., pp. 9-10.

employer, embodying the phenomenon of the transformation of a job into an independent activity, which causes the employer to disappear. The other axis, which goes in the opposite direction, is the employer with no jobs. In this second situation the employer exists, but he hires people only for a limited time, for a given task, for a temporary engagement; there is recruitment, but not employment. The employer's period of commitment is limited in advance, as well as the extent of his obligations in relation to those pertaining to the typical employment situation. Under the heading of "employers with no jobs" one could classify fixed-term contracts, part-time working (which is liable to forfeit the employment protection which a traditional employment contract confers), temporary contracts, job-training contracts, and home-based working and teleworking in cases where these last two are equivalent to salaried employment. Under the heading of "jobs with no employer", where we see another manifestation of the externalisation of the workforce which this time conceals the employer, one may place self-employed working, fake subcontracting, and work in the black economy.

THE EMPLOYER WITH NO JOBS

THE FIXED-TERM EMPLOYMENT CONTRACT

In all countries one finds an expansion of this kind of employment contract, which was rare and exceptional up to the beginning of the 1970s. The trade unions were against the idea of accepting this type of employment, because it deprives the workers of certain protective measures as regards dismissal. It also deprives them of other rights such as seniority, and hinders the exercise of their collective rights. In some countries such as France, Germany and Spain (and in Portugal as early as 1974) one finds a sort of consecration of fixed-term contracts in new legal regulations.

It should be pointed out that the fixed-term contract appears also under several new forms: fixed-term contracts not only for seasonal work, but also for precise work, task-based work, job-creation situations and the start-up of new activities. This new formula, and the practice of temporary work, have institutionalised job insecurity.

The Federal Republic of Germany

German law, while allowing fixed-term employment contracts[5], at the same time used to lay down certain conditions (which were in effect restrictions) worked out by case-law to avoid any exploitation of this form of contract.

According to the Federal Labour Court[6], any limitation on the duration of an employment contract must correspond to a reasonable cause, justified in fact. The concept of an objective cause is not defined precisely by case-law, but a series of situations have been worked out which are considered as objective causes.

Thus there is an acceptance that fixed-term contracts may be drawn up when an employer needs auxiliary workers to replace salaried staff who are ill, or when the employer needs to set up a trial period (which must not exceed six months); the same applies in cases of the employment of artists (musicians, singers, actors) or seasonal jobs. The objective cause justifying this kind of contract also applies in cases of termination of funding (known in advance) for a university research programme, or in the case of a teacher engaged by a school which is facing a situation of permanent staff reductions.

In cases where the reason is not objectively valid, and also when it is not possible to specify the duration of the contract, the contract is held to have been made for an indeterminate period.[7] Now, the employment promotion law of 26 April 1985 has suspended the principles of case-law just cited, until 1 January 1990.[8] In effect, article 1, paragraph 1, of the employment promotion law suppresses during this period the requirement for an objective cause for all workers employed in a firm for the first time. In this case, a single limitation of duration, which is not to exceed eighteen months, is permitted. In all other cases, with the exception of a new recruitment, the criteria worked out by case-law must be respected.

The law on employment promotion encourages, in a general way, a growth in the number of employees having an unstable employment

---

5. For an overall approach to the case-law in question, see Schaub, *Arbeitsrechtshandbuch*, 5. Auflage, par. 39 II.

6. BAG AP nr.16, par.620 BGB fixed-term contract.

7. BAG AP nr.60, par.620 BGB fixed-term contract. Däubler, "Crise, maintien de l'emploi et partage du travail", Geneva, Georg, 1984, p. 25; Falkenberg, "Atypische Arbeitsverhältnisse in her BRD", 11th international conference of the International Society for Labour Law and Social Security, Caracas, 17-20 September 1985.

8. M. Lowisch, "Das Beschäftigungsförderungsgesetz", 1985, *Betriebs Berater*, p. 18, 1985; W. Däubler, Martine Friant: "Un récent exemple de flexibilisation législative: la loi allemande pour la promotion de l'emploi du 26 avril 1985", *Droit Social*, no. 9/10, 1986.

relationship and receiving reduced protection, through the provisions already described, and it contains, at the same time, other more specific provisions with the aim of encouraging recruitment in small and medium-sized companies. It states in fact that a firm which has been set up for less than six months and employs fewer than 20 people may make employment contracts with a duration of 24 months.

France

The example of the fixed-term contract in France clearly shows both the law's hesitations when faced with new forms, and its oscillation caused by fluctuating political majorities, but it also shows the difficulty of the provisions which it is proposed to incorporate with the permanent provisions of the labour code.[9]

Although the civil code states that one may only engage one's services "for a time or for a certain company", in 1979 the law facilitated the adoption of fixed-term contracts. It decided to look in the same way on contracts with a precise expiry date and on contracts with an undefined term corresponding to a defined task. In 1982, the law limited the cases in which it is possible to recruit within the framework of a fixed-term contract. In 1985 there was a further intervention to extend the number of cases for the adoption of fixed-term contracts. Lastly came Order no. 86.248 of 11 August 1986, which continues the trend towards complete contractual freedom. The new principle is that a fixed-term contract may be concluded freely, on the sole condition that it must correspond to a precise task. The word "task" stands in contrast to the word "job": the law prohibits contracts intended to make a durable arrangement for a job linked to the permanent and normal activities of the companies. The requirement for a definite term, stated in advance, disappears in the following cases:

- temporary absence or suspension of contract of a worker (illness, maternity, paid holidays);

- jobs which are temporary by nature, i.e. seasonal jobs (hotels, food processing, agricultural production);

- when there is recourse to fixed-term contracts in order to alleviate the unemployment crisis: long-term unemployed workers, young people aged under 25.

---

9. See G. Lyon-Caen, "Notes sur quelques nouvelles formes d'emploi", pp. 1-7.

The fixed-term contract must be written down, and it must include a precise definition of its object, the expiry date of the term (where a precise date has been fixed), and so forth. When the contract is to run for an imprecise term, the parties must set a minimum duration, which they determine freely.

During the period of this contract, employees have the same rights as workers recruited through an open-ended contract, whether one is speaking of legal rights, established by law or by agreement; or of rights arising from professional custom; or of collective rights. French law guarantees compensation for dismissal, under certain conditions, for employees recruited on fixed-term contract. The contract for this category ceases producing the effect of full rights at its expiry date, without the employer being obliged to give advance notice. It can also be renewed when the expiry date arrives, without losing its character as a "fixed-term contract". However:

- only two renewals are allowed;

- a renewal may not be made for a duration exceeding that of the original contract;

- the renewal must not exceed the maximum duration, set at 24 months.

If any one of these conditions is not observed, and if contractual relations continue between the employer and the employee after the expiry date has elapsed, then the contract becomes an open-ended employment contract.

Italy

In Italy, fixed-term contracts of employment were first regulated by law no. 230 of 1962, which permits the use of this type of contract only in clearly defined cases, listed exclusively as: seasonal working, replacement of an absent worker, work of a special nature, the entertainment industry. The provisions of this law have been applied by case-law in a restrictive way, and this has induced the legislators to intervene again in order to facilitate the use of fixed-term contracts of employment in certain cases. There has been an increase in the number of criteria. On the basis of laws no. 918 of 3.2.1978 and no. 598 of 26.11.1979, recourse to these contracts has become possible in cases where the company is overloaded for a short period, in sectors where employers face peak periods: tourism, commerce, services.

The latest legislative reform, however, according to Bruno

Veneziani[10], has "changed some basic principles" on which Italian labour law used to stand, and now favours fixed-term contracts. In effect, law no. 79 of 25.3.1983 allows for the extension of authorisation to other sectors of the economy, while law no. 273 of 1984 allows for its extension to women workers. The consequence of this has been to expand that portion of the labour market which uses fixed-term contracts, at the expense of the open-ended employment contract, which means at the expense of traditional employment relationships. It should be noted that in Italy the law gives some control to the trade union movement — the most representative trade union organisations — and to the administrative authorities — the labour inspectorate — over whether particular companies should have recourse to fixed-term contracts. While the employer's powers in relation to using this category of atypical employment appear to be limited, one might wonder on the other hand what this means in terms of the extent and significance of "neo-corporatism" within the Italian trade union movement.

Portugal

In Portugal, there is an unprecedented use of fixed-term contracts of employment. It is estimated that 66% of all employment contracts signed belong to the category of fixed-term contracts.[11] Thus, two workers out of every three recruited in recent years have been taken on for a limited duration, and about one-sixth of all employees in companies are working under fixed-term contracts. In some sectors such as textiles, building and the electronics industry, there are firms which almost exclusively employ this category of workers with no security.

This type of contract is regulated by legislative decree no. 781 of 28.10.1976 which, on the one hand, limits the possibility of dismissal by comparison with previous law, while on the other hand encouraging the use of fixed-term contracts of employment. Such a contract must be drawn up in writing, and must specify a duration which is not to exceed six months, as well as the conditions under which the task is to be performed. The contract may be renewed when it reaches the expiry date. But successive renewals must not exceed the maximum duration set by the legislators, which is three years.

---

10. See national report, pp. 2-3.

11. See Antonio Monteiro Fernandes, *Les relations d'emploi atypiques au Portugal*, p. 7; but the author admits some reservations as to the reliability and accuracy of the statistical data. These reservations do not, however, prevent one from seeing the basic trends.

The law considers as null and void any term of the contract which "has as its aim a derogation from the provisions which govern open-ended contracts". This is a provision which in practice is rarely applied.

Employees on a fixed-term contract, as a rule, come under the collective agreements applied to traditional employees, and have the same working conditions. As trade union members, they enjoy the same rights as the traditional employees, although their collective rights are not identical. In fact, these temporary workers do not have the right to be members of the staff council ("comissões de trabalhadores") which represents the workers at company level. According to law no. 40 of 1979, only permanent employees are entitled to be elected. If one considers, first of all, the importance of the responsibilities and functions exercised by this representative organ — "management control" — of the company, the right to a wide range of information, the right to obligatory consultations on the most important company decisions, the right to become involved in the reorganisation of production units and the right to draw up company plans, and if one considers, secondly, the very high proportion of workers on fixed-term contracts, then one can see that this element of discrimination affects the non-permanent workers in a very negative way. It should be noted, finally, that the end of the validity of the contract does not arise simply from the mere fact that the expiry date has been reached: a declaration is required from the employer, indicating that he or she does not wish to renew the contract.

Spain

In Spain too, by means of the recent reform of the Estatuto de los Trabajadores, effected in law no. 32 of 1984, the fixed-term contract of employment has emerged from its limited status within the framework of existing legislation, to be encouraged with the launch of a new type of fixed-term contract. According to article 15 of the relevant law, the new development is the fixed-term contract "for the purpose of launching a new activity" on the part of new or established companies for which the traditional type of contract would act as a restraint. This new type of contract offers them a sort of "trial period". The maximum duration of such a contract is three years. It is also permitted to use fixed-term contracts when taking on unemployed workers, without any requirement to state an objective cause (decree no. 1989 of 1984). The minimum duration of the contract is six months, while the maximum duration can range up to six years. The worker is entitled to compensation on the expiry of the contract.

Greece

In Greece, considerable use is made of fixed-term contracts. This is the type of contract used to cover all forms of atypical employment — intermittent, occasional, temporary, on call — including seasonal work such as tourism, restaurants, teaching (especially of foreign languages), fur workers, etc.

Fixed-term contracts are governed by the Greek civil code, and by an old set of regulations dating from the 1920s. According to the code, the fixed-term contract, or definite duration contract, may have a written form or not, and is drawn up between the two parties in cases where the duration of the job is limited by the nature of the work or because of special conditions. As the relevant provisions do not define the term "conditions", these conditions have been defined by case-law, with a great deal of flexibility. The duration may be set on an annual, monthly, weekly or even daily basis. The contract may be part-time, and connected with a precise job, a particular season, etc.

When the contract comes to the end of its duration, the employer's only responsibility is to report the end of the contract to the bureau of employment and unemployment. The contract can also be ended prematurely "for a grave reason", duly announced by one or other party. In practice, employers very frequently use this procedure. In cases of repeated renewals of a fixed-term contract — there are no limits — this can become an open-ended contract in cases where its duration is not justified by its nature and where that limited duration was expressly designed to "frustrate the law". This concept is rather hazy in Greek law, and it is up to the judge to decide when a fixed-term contract, renewed on several occasions, may be reclassified as a typical employment contract. (In a recent judgement, despite thirty successive renewals of a fixed-term contract, this was not held to be an open-ended contract.) In such a case the employer is obliged, among other things, to pay out at the end of the contract the same legal compensation laid down for the dismissal of workers in a typical employment relationship.

Given that the use of fixed-term contracts has become very widespread in recent years, many company unions have demanded that the practice be stopped because, in the case cited, it was not justified by its objective, it prevented the worker from integrating into the firm, and deprived him of his right to stability of employment and his legal right to compensation in case of dismissal. This claim did not succeed: the Greek law in this area guarantees all the flexibility required for companies pleading the economic crisis.

Netherlands

In the Netherlands the situation is comparable with Greece: fixed-term contracts are governed by a set of provisions in the Dutch civil code, dating from 1907. These provisions do not impose any limitation on the employer in using fixed-term contracts; those limitations are provided for in collective agreements.

When the fixed-term contract draws to its end on the agreed date, it expires by force of law, and none of the various protections against dismissal applies. However, when notice is required either by individual or by collective agreement, then all the legal protections against dismissal can be invoked. This is not infrequently the case. When a fixed-term contract is renewed within a month, at the end of the renewed contract all the normal protections of the open-ended contracts are applied. Case-law tends to interpret these provisions strictly.

PART-TIME WORKING

Recognition and generalisation following legislative action

Part-time working is undergoing a considerable boom at the moment because, while presenting itself as the sole possibility of joining the labour force for certain categories of workers, it simultaneously matches a very high level of demand on the part of employers. The decrease in the daily duration of work has meant that employees work with greater intensity — in principle without any extra pay — and a part-time contract allows an employer to achieve better workforce management. One of the results of this demand for part-time working is a wide range of laws and new regulations in the majority of member states which are adopted in order to deal with this new form of work, which already existed without being as important as it is today.

The rise in the number of workers may be observed in all member states, independently of whether there has been an "updating" of the law on this long-established form of employment, and independently of the attitude of the trade unions towards it — an attitude which, in certain countries such as Denmark and Greece, remains hostile. In these cases, one still finds a total rejection of the "legitimation" of this kind of work which, according to those unions, should remain the exception, because it does not provide sufficient protection for workers. In other countries, the union position is much less trenchant, although the positions of the main union confederations (socialist, communist, christian and liberal) in the same country may not converge (for example, Italy, France, Belgium). The main proposal of the European trade unions was — and still is for most of them — that working time should in general be reduced. But a large number of them accept this new form of work on condition that it is freely chosen and that it is accompanied by sufficient protection: equality of remuneration, and so forth.

The number of part-time workers varies from country to country, and it is not always easy to obtain the exact percentage in relation to the total number of workers. The only people recorded are those who work enough hours to be taken into account by the law, the social security system and the statistics. But the average percentage in member states must certainly exceed 15% of workers, the vast majority of whom (over 85%) are female. In certain countries, such as Denmark and the United Kingdom, half the total number of active women are employed on a part-time contract: in Denmark the figure is 50% and in Britain it is 45%. It is obvious that this form of organisation of working time makes it possible to reconcile the demands of family responsibilities and professional activity. Men who work part-time are normally elderly, handicapped or very young workers (such as students). However, in recent years it has been found that "normal" workers, not elderly, not very young, not handicapped, not female, find themselves obliged — for reasons due both to the economic crisis and to the introduction of new technology — to change over from a full-time to a part-time employment relationship. The persistence of the phenomenon, and also a government policy favourable to it, has led to the revision of regulations on part-time working, already mentioned, in the following countries: the Federal Republic of Germany (1985), Belgium (1981), Spain (1984), France (1984), Italy (1984) and Portugal (1984).

Part-time working may appear in the guise of a reduced work timetable, but also in the form of a job done on certain days of the week, under the guise of job-sharing, alternating working, or possibly pre-retirement combined with an unemployed person working part-time. The characteristic feature is the regular performance of an activity for a number of hours fewer than the number which is considered normal.

The path of collective bargaining

● *The Federal Republic of Germany*

In the Federal Republic of Germany, while the part-time employee works in a more intensive manner than a full-time worker, weak union representation means that he or she receives a salary lower than that corresponding to the duration of his or her work.[12] Deprived of compensation for extra hours worked, by virtue of the case-law prevailing at the Federal Labour Tribunal,[13] the part-time employee is also excluded from old age and illness insurance as well as unemployment insurance if the duration of his or her work, and possibly also the salary paid, are lower than a threshold expressly cited in the social code (Sozialgesetzbuch, IV).[14]

Although it aims to make part-time working more attractive, the 1985 law on employment promotion (BeschG) has not really improved the workers' lot.[15] This law certainly states (paragraph 2 subsection 1) that the employer is obliged to treat part-time workers in the same way as full-time workers "unless objective reasons justify different treatment". Recognised for a long time by the courts, this principle was not accompanied by a specific regulation on the question of discrimination against women, although they represent 90% of part-time workers in the Federal Republic of Germany. The law leaves it to the courts to determine the objective reasons which could justify different treatment, thus permitting alterations in the principle of equality of treatment between part-time and full-time workers.[16]

● *Spain*

Spain was the first among the current member states to recognise and regulate part-time working through legislation. In fact, article 12 of the Estatuto de los Trabajadores, the most important of Spain's labour laws, passed in March 1980, states that a part-time worker is somebody who does his or her job in a set number of hours per day which is less than two-thirds of the normal working day.[17] This first tentative recognition was followed by another set of regulations which went much further in removing obstacles to the development of part-

---

12. W. Däubler, in "Crise, maintien de l'emploi et partage du travail", loc. cit., pp. 126 ff.

13. BAG, *Betriebs Berater*, 1977, p. 596; see also critiques of the legal literature: Schaub, *Arbeitsrechtshandbuch*, vol. 1, par. 44 III 2; W. Däubler, *Das Arbeitsrecht* 2, 2nd edition, Reinbeck, 1981, p. 407.

14. According to paragraph 8 subsection 1 number 1 of the social code I IV, part-time workers employed for less than 15 hours per week, and with an income of under 416 DM per month, are not covered by illness and old age insurance, while workers employed for less than 19 hours per week are excluded from the unemployment insurance system.

15. M. Lowisch, "Beschäftigungsförderungsgesetz", *Betriebs Berater*, 1985, op. cit.; W. Däubler - M. Friant, op. cit., note 19. A recent example of flexibilisation: the German employment protection law of 26 April 1985, op. cit.

16. W. Däubler - M. Friant, op. cit.

17. M.A. Olea, Report on Spanish law at the Geneva colloquium, loc. cit. pp. 99 ff.

time working.[18] The new regulations now envisage a reduced number of working hours calculated on a daily, weekly or monthly basis, but not on an annual basis. No minimum duration is prescribed. Law no. 32/84 (see also 1991, 30 October 1984) which introduces the new regulations calls for the application of the principle of equality and proportionality between part-time and full-time workers; part-time workers enjoy the rights conferred by the social security system in proportion to the amount of working time done. The "contrato de trabajo a tiempo parcial" — which must in principle be concluded for an open-ended period, and can only be made for a limited period in certain cases laid down in the legislation on full-time employment — has to be drawn up in writing, and must contain obligatory clauses relating to the nature and duration of the contract and the number of working hours and days. It must also be registered at the employment office. The decree also specifies that it is possible for both parties to agree on a transfer, in accordance with the provisions of existing collective agreements, from a full-time to a part-time contract. It should be pointed out that, since part-time working has not become as widespread in Spain as in countries like the United Kingdom or the Federal Republic of Germany, these regulations often express the aims and policies of the Spanish government, which are concerned not so much with "normalising" part-time working, but rather with promoting its expansion.

● *France*

In France, this atypical form of work was regulated for the first time by Order no. 82-271 of 26 March 1982, which specifies the companies that can use part-time working, the employees who can work part-time, and the form and content of the contract. It also regulates the conditions for the duration of part-time work, which cannot exceed a weekly or monthly ceiling equal to four-fifths of the statutory or agreed work period. Although the law fixes a maximum period, no minimum is laid down. Through the regulations for part-time work, the general rules concerning social security contributions and the calculation of numbers of staff are waived.[19] Thus, the contributions paid for two half-time employees will not be higher than those paid

---

18. Federico Durn Lopez, *Modalidades de contratation laboral*, Madrid, 1986, pp. 36 ff. On the 1984 reform, see the Spanish report presented to the "Journées d'études sur les pays du Sud de l'Europe", organised by the Assocation française d'études des relations professionnelles, Paris, April 1986.

19. See J. Pelissier, "La relation de travail atypique" (French report presented to Caracas conference), loc. cit., pp. 531 ff; J.C. Javillier, "Crise, maintien de l'emploi et partage du travail - France", Geneva colloquium, loc. cit., pp. 126 ff. See J. Pelissier, loc. cit., p. 533.

for one full-time employee if the total of the two half-time wages is equal to one full-time wage. As regards the minimum period, it should be pointed out that there is a provision for employees who want to qualify for social security benefits, enabling them to demand that their employers give them a sufficient number of hours (the aggregate of two or more part-time jobs) to meet the social security requirements.

Part-time employees benefit from all the collective rights to which full-time employees are entitled. They can vote, and are eligible for office, in elections to appoint staff representatives and works councils. Part-time employees are included in the company's total staff numbers, but in proportion to the ratio between the timetables specified in the work contract of the plant, where the period of work is less than 20 hours per week or 80 hours per month. Companies enjoy considerable freedom in allocating working time, on a daily, weekly or monthly basis, or over even longer periods. Another form of atypical work has also emerged: alternating work. This is organised by airlines: aircrew who so wish may work one month, take the next month off, and then return to work one or two months. Although this solution lies outside the scope of the provisions on part-time employment, it works on the same principle, and is not illegal. Problems arise, however, in connection with the calculation of staff totals and the payment of social security contributions, which may also become complicated because of the fact that the employees, by agreement, receive no remuneration or other compensation during the period when they are not working.

● *Italy*

Until very recently, part-time working in Italy was encouraged neither by the trade unions nor by the legislators. The number of workers with part-time contracts was restricted mainly to small and medium-sized companies. The legal basis for these contracts was the principle of contractual autonomy and the right to engage freely in work. Since there was a substantial increase in the demand for this kind of contract by a certain number of large firms, a new law was promulgated (law no. 863 of 19.12.1984) to regulate these contracts.[20] Workers wishing to work on a half-time basis must register, and indicate the type of work and the timetable involved. Collective agreements which regulate part-time working in detail in Italy must state the precise conditions whereby a full-time contract may become a part-time one.

---

20. Edoardo Ghera, *Diritto del lavoro*, op. cit., pp. 315-316, and report to the Geneva colloquium, loc. cit., pp. 182-183.

Part-time workers are counted as members of the staff, and enjoy social security rights in proportion to the amount of work done.

In all member states, part-time working is spreading through the medium of collective bargaining, notably at company level. In certain member states such as England, Ireland and Denmark, collective bargaining is the only method of regulation.

● *United Kingdom*

In the United Kingdom part-time workers are the most numerous group of atypical workers,[21] numbering more than four and a half million workers. Of these 45% are female — the overwhelming majority being married women — while 15% are mainly workers approaching retirement age. But given that the percentage of full-time male workers is falling, a process of mild "de-feminisation" has started for this category of workers.

The Department of Employment considers people working at least 30 hours per week as part-time workers, but for the purposes of labour law — since 1975 and the adoption of new rules — the threshold is 16 hours per week; this may even be reduced to 8 hours per week in cases where a person has been working for five years. The legal status of part-time workers in the United Kingdom is uncertain. During the 1980s, studies carried out on this category of workers[22] have shown that they receive very low salaries, that most of them are ineligible for paid holidays and health insurance, that they are often excluded from pension rights, that they have no chance of training or promotion. The findings of the studies in question, which were carried out with regard to women's employment and the inequalities and discriminations which they face, have contributed to the growing of the marked imbalance which exists between the rights of full-time workers and those of part-time workers. The British trade unions, in their concern to share out the available jobs, seem to favour[23] rather than rule out part-time working. At the same time,

---

21. See Patricia Leighton, "New Forms and Aspects of Atypical Employment Relationships - The Law and Practice in the United Kingdom" (British report to the Caracas conference), p. 314; Paul Davies and Mark Freedland, *Labour Law Text and Materials*, same publisher, London, 1984, pp. 100 ff.; William Wedderburn, *Workers and the Law*, 3rd edition, London, 1986, pp. 116 ff; NEDO (J. Attinson, Nigel Meager), *Changing Working Patterns: how companies achieve flexibility to meet new needs*, London, 1986, pp. 22 ff.

22. See O. Robinson and J. Wallace, *Part-time Employment and Sex Discrimination Legislation in Great Britain*, Department of Employment (Research Paper no.43), London, 1984.

23. Of course this depends on the individual company involved, and sometimes one finds staunch resistance against the introduction of atypical working; see for example NEDO, *Changing Working Patterns*, op. cit., p. 25.

they are campaigning to ensure that the workers involved have the same rights as their full-time colleagues.

One should note the extraordinary level of introduction of part-time working through collective bargaining at company level.[24] Undoubtedly, a number of companies in financial difficulty are cutting their proportion of typical employment contracts, thus reducing the hard core of full-time workers, and replacing them by part-time or temporary contracts, with union agreement. But other companies, experiencing no such problems, are also opting for a new personnel policy and management, leading to company agreements with the following content: the company agrees that it will not lay off workers for a three-year period, and the union agrees that the company may recruit 30% of its staff under an atypical contract (a part-time or temporary contract).[25]

● *Denmark*

In Denmark, part-time working — widely known and practised — is regulated by collective bargaining; in this sense the legal status of part-time workers is monitored by the trade unions. Many collective agreements, especially in sectors typically associated with women workers, allow part-time working. If the collective agreement does not contain an explicit special provision, the prevailing view in the legal literature is that part-time working is forbidden.

● *Netherlands*

In the Netherlands, on the contrary, employers are free to offer part-time contracts, and this is in fact widely done: currently 25% of all employment is fulfilled by part-time work (75% of part-time workers are women). The government promotes this development as part of its drive to reduce unemployment. In general, the labour conditions of part-time workers are the same as those of full-time workers, although some conspicuous discriminations survive.

---

24. In certain sectors, such as retail trading, part-time working is the dominant form of employment, and is still growing. The staff is divided into three groups, as follows: "hard-core" staff, who hold the key positions with career prospects (most of this group are men); the part-time workers (mostly women) mainly working during the midday peak hours; and the temporary staff, young boys and girls (often students) who are taken on for a short time during the week and especially at the weekend. This division of category and gender is to be found in companies of the same type in the majority of member states; see inter alia NEDO, *Changing Working Patterns*, p. 25.

25. See the cases cited by W.E. Wedderburn, *Workers and the Law*, op. cit., p. 117. One does find clauses in British company agreements granting priority to part-time workers in seeking a full-time contract.

Special cases: Greece and Portugal

Part-time working appears in a slightly different guise in Greece and Portugal. These two countries have experience of part-time working as an atypical form of employment which is undoubtedly growing; but given the peculiarities of the employment market in Greece and Portugal, part-time working appears mainly as a second job, carried on alongside one's principal employment, and hence not always declared to the authorities. Part-time working as a main employment, being subject to legal regulations, is very limited.

- *Greece: sought by government and industrialists, but rejected by the trade unions*

In Greece, there are no special regulations for part-time working. In any case, we do not know the precise extent or function of this atypical form of employment, which certainly exists and which is posing legal problems which have not yet been properly worked out, although Greek case-law is attempting to deal with them.[26]

While the ratio of part-time workers officially declared is perhaps the lowest in any member state, the reality of part-time working is very different. It appears in Greece, as we have seen, under the guise of a job parallel to the main employment, especially widespread in the services sector. During the last few years, however, part-time working as a main employment itself has grown, especially in the public utility companies (which are state-owned) such as the electricity company, the telephone and telegraph company, but also in banking and insurance. It is not reduced and proportional to the hours worked. Part-time workers are paid on an hourly basis ("horomisthion"). They are obliged to register with the social security system, only in cases where "they are earning enough to live on their work", and in practice they are deprived of annual holidays. Some years ago the uncertainty and incompleteness of the legal status of part-time working was demonstrated,[27] and in fact the current legal system impedes the development of "work by the hour", as it is called in Greece.

Recently the Greek government has stated its intention of moving towards a legal settlement of the part-time working situation — which has long been demanded by Greek industrialists — in order to

---

26. One notes a shortage of studies and statistics, as well as a lack of discussion in the legal literature, on questions relating to part-time working. See Nikitas Aliprantis, ''Le travail à temps partiel selon le droit de travail grec: analyse critique de ses questions fondamentales'', in *Droit et Politique*, no.3, Salonika, 1982, pp. 267 ff.

27. See N. Aliprantis, loc. cit.

encourage the sharing of available employment, especially in the industrial sector. On 30 July 1986 a meeting of ESAP, the National Development and Planning Council, discussed the twelve points put forward by the Economics Minister to promote jobs and counteract unemployment. The measures to encourage part-time working were planned initially for the public sector alone, but were later proposed for the private sector too. The other questions related to early retirement in the private sector, a ban on employing retired persons, shiftworking, parental leave, and payment on an hourly basis ("horomisthion"). The Greek trade unions expressed their formal opposition, on the grounds that one now finds part-time working being used less as a means of "sharing out employment" than as a new company management policy (particularly in multinational firms — for example, TWA is laying off half of its employees, and then taking them on again with a part-time contract).

Part-time working simply requires an agreement between the two parties, without any formalities such as written contracts. The written form is required, however, for alternating (intermittent) working, as envisaged and regulated by Greek law (law no. 2961/1954). Once an employee is working part-time, whether by implicit or explicit agreement, he or she is only entitled to remuneration.

● *Portugal: unknown in its modern form*

In Portugal part-time working, well-known and relatively widespread, has been recognised and regulated by a legal decree of 1971. But for the moment this type of working is carried out in a very different context from what happens in other member states. One of the objectives of this atypical form is, as in the Greek case, to increase the income of certain workers. These are people who already have a principal job, but whose income is insufficient for their needs. This category of "part-timers" is not covered by the law, and it is by no means easy, moreover, to obtain adequate data on the approximate numbers involved and the nature of their work.

Another category of part-time workers is that envisaged by legal decree no.409 of 27 September 1971, which recommends and regulates this type of employment for (a) female workers with family obligations; (b) workers with limited working capacity (handicapped); (c) students studying either in high schools or in higher educational establishments. Thus, it cannot be considered that the regulations in this area envisage part-time working as a means of encouraging the sharing of available employment.[28]

---

28. Antonio Monteiro Fernandes, *Les relations d'emploi atypique.*

Other forms of part-time working: job-sharing — a full-time job divided between two or more workers

Job-sharing, the splitting of a full-time job between two or more workers who take a proportionate share in the remuneration and benefits, is undoubtedly a new form of work in the European Community.[29] This is a form of part-time working in the broad sense of the term, but it appears to raise its own set of legal problems. Job-sharing is not in fact recognised by labour law in all member states. It is accepted by the legal systems of countries such as Britain, Ireland, the Netherlands and Belgium, and it is not ruled out by Italian law; French law has nothing to say on the matter. On the other hand, it is regulated in detail by the recent German law (1985) on employment promotion (BeschG), and is not classified as legal in countries such as France and Spain. Job-sharing is almost unknown in Portugal. This is a type of work organisation which comes up against very strong cultural obstacles: the very notion of sharing a job runs counter to the tradition of "job ownership", reinforced by recent legislation on dismissals. The introduction of this new form of work only seems feasible after legislative action.

In any case, even where it is accepted, job-sharing (a concept which covers very different practices in different countries) raises many problems which are far from being resolved. In practice job-sharing, although quite similar to part-time working, is distinguished by the fact that the job being shared requires a certain level of qualification, implies a certain degree of responsibility, may offer career prospects, and demands some co-operation and contact, usually outside working hours, between the persons sharing the post.

This new form[30] came to Europe from North America. It made its appearance at a time when circumstances were not yet favourable. Its objective was to improve the quality of working life for workers unwilling or unable to work full-time. The overwhelming majority of workers sharing a job were then, as they are now, women with family commitments and especially women with children.[31]

---

29. Barney Olmsted, "Un nouveau style de travail fait son apparition: le partage des emplois," *Revue Internationale du Travail*, vol.118, May-June 1979, pp. 300 ff.; Joyce Epstein, *Issues in Job-Sharing* (which provides a full bibliography); Hortense Horburger, "Job-sharing, Probleme und Möglichkeiten" (1985), presented in *Europe Sociale*, 2/86, pp. 93 ff.

30. Actually, it is not an entirely new form of work organisation. The idea was very widespread in the 1930s, during the Depression, but the practice of job-sharing was also found in many companies which used this measure on a provisional basis in order to avoid mass redundancies.

31. Men are less likely to accept job-sharing; they are hostile to the very idea, which does not suit the social customs of male employment (see Epstein, loc. cit., p. 53: "giving up a job is not considered masculine"). One does however find young men sharing jobs

Among member states, one finds job-sharing more particularly in the United Kingdom, Ireland and perhaps in the Federal Republic of Germany. Other countries such as Italy, the Netherlands, Belgium, Denmark and Spain have this form of employment, but to a rather limited extent. One finds it also in France — where it may be much more widespread than it seems — and in Greece, although here it is a very exceptional arrangement. The sectors favouring job-sharing are mostly banking, insurance and teaching.

● *Job-sharing in Germany*

In the Federal Republic of Germany, the law on job promotion considerably eases the problems associated with this specific form of part-time working, giving it full legal status.[32]

This type of contract had previously meant that any worker sharing a job was obliged to do all the work if the other partner in the job-sharing arrangement was absent. The new law put an end to this obligation. According to article 1, paragraph 5 subsection 1, in each particular case there must be a specific contractual agreement. A general obligation to provide replacement can be envisaged in the employment contract only exceptionally, if it is confined to cases of urgent necessity for the company. In such cases the employee is only obliged to perform replacement duties if this can reasonably be expected of him or her.

In cases of the dismissal or resignation of one partner, the employer used to be entitled to dismiss the other partner as well, to recruit a new team. The 1985 law has ruled out such action, and now the employer only has the right to transfer the remaining worker.

● *Job-sharing to create part-time jobs for the unemployed*

In certain countries such as the United Kingdom, the Netherlands, Belgium, and recently Greece, there is official encouragement to divide a full-time post into two part-time jobs, one of which goes to a registered unemployed person, and there are special incentives for employers who facilitate this possibility. In Spain, Belgium, Greece, Luxembourg and elsewhere, this same method has been adopted, in combination with the possibility of early retirement for elderly workers in certain circumstances.

---

because they want to have free time. Then there are quite exceptional cases such as the two personnel managers of a Belgian furnishing company, who have held this post since 1981 (see *Le Soir*, 8 April 1986).

32. On the problems in question, see Hoyningen Huene, "Rechtliche Gestaltungsmöglichkeiten beim Job Sharing Arbeitsverhältnis," *Betriebs Berater*, 1982, p. 1240.

i) The replacement contract in Spain:
a case of job-sharing between an elderly worker and a young unemployed person

The "replacement contract" was first envisaged in article 12 of the Workers' Charter, and was later updated in reforming decree 1991 of 1984. Such a contract is drawn up in cases where a worker approaching retirement age, and fulfilling all the other legal conditions for receiving a pension except for the age requirement (3 years), agrees to work half-time and give the other half of the job to another worker. But this other worker must be an unemployed person registered at the employment office. The "replacement contract" must be drawn up in writing and must give the name, age and grade of the worker being replaced. The duration of the contract cannot extend beyond the day when the worker being replaced reaches retirement age. The worker being replaced may request and receive 50% of his or her pension while awaiting retirement, and also receive half of his or her salary during the same period. The objective is to promote employment. If the employer decides, when the "replacement contract" comes to an end, to transform it into a full-time open-ended contract, then the employer has to pay only half of the social security contributions during the entire duration of the new "transformed" contract.

ii) Belgium:
job-sharing as a means of early retirement

It should be emphasised that in Belgium the social law of 1 August 1983, while following the same logic (giving elderly workers the option of retiring, thus encouraging the employment of workers who find themselves unemployed), goes a little further: it allows an elderly worker to change over at the age of 60 from conventional early retirement to actual retirement. The condition is that the employer must agree to replace the retired worker with two workers employed half-time.[33] This is admittedly not job-sharing in the true sense; we do not have, as in the Spanish case, the combination of a young worker and a worker close to retirement, sharing the same job. Instead, there are two separate and independent half-time jobs.

iii) Greece:
job-sharing as a means of retirement will be tried

In Greece, job-sharing to create part-time jobs for unemployed people has been adopted within the framework of measures taken by the

---

33. See article 85 of the law of 1 August 1983, and the report by Eliane Vogel, p. 45.

government and designed to encourage new job creation. Workers aged over 60, or those over 55 who are not yet entitled to retirement may, with the employer's agreement, continue working on a part-time basis. The duration of the work must not be less than four hours per day. In this case, the employer must take on a worker who is officially registered as unemployed and entitled to unemployment benefits, to do the other half of the job. Social contributions are paid by the employer and the elderly worker, in proportion to the hours worked, whereas those payable on behalf of the unemployed person who is working part-time are completely covered by the national employment agency (OAED). The workers in question are forbidden to take on a second job.

This is an experimental measure; the government will evaluate its results after six months, and then decide whether to keep it going.

iv) Career breaks in favour of the unemployed, and switching over to half-time working

Legislators are showing proof of imagination: a way has to be found, if not to share out employment, then at least to ensure some degree of interchange between employment and unemployment. This is the position in all countries; here we may simply note two possibilities allowed by Belgian law.

"Career breaks" are allowed by the Belgian recovery law of 25 January 1985 and the royal decree accompanying it, which are concerned particularly with part-time workers; they may request the total suspension of their activities for a minimum duration of six months, and a maximum duration of twelve months, in order to yield their place to a totally unemployed person in receipt of benefit. In such cases, the worker accepting the suspension receives additional remuneration, a suspension payment proportional to the time worked. This is one of several experimental measures taken in Belgium in recent times which will either disappear or be continued according to the needs of the situation[34].

v) Facilitating an alternative for the unemployed

Belgian law also allows a full-time worker who has been working for at least one year to reduce his or her professional activity and give half of it over to a totally unemployed person in receipt of benefit.[35]

---

34. After an order decided on by the Council of Ministers; see article 4 of the royal decree of 25 January 1985, and the report by Eliane Vogel.

35. See Article 5 of the Royal Decree of 25 January 1985, and the Report of Elaine Vogel.

In this case, a supplementary allocation is added to his or her remuneration, which is doubled for workers aged over 50.

It is also worth drawing attention here to the Luxembourg law of 28 March 1987 on early retirement, which lays down a complete policy of early retirement and envisages, inter alia, the possibility of "solidarity pre-retirement". This form of early retirement has to be authorised by the employer, within the framework of a special agreement. In this case, the Employment Fund will repay 50% of the cost to the employer, on condition that the employer takes on one or more persons seeking work and registered with the manpower services, with either an open-ended contract or an apprenticeship contract.

TEMPORARY EMPLOYMENT

> ... Who were able to take away the horizon
> from in front of your eyes — and nothing but the
> horizon, leaving everything else visible....
>
> H. Michaux, *Au pays de la Magie*

Contracts with several employers:
the expansion of "triangular" relationships

In all member countries one finds an expansion in "triangular" employment relationships, expressed through temporary employment contracts, through subcontracting, through personnel transfers, and through other even more modern and unfamiliar forms: labour pools (in the Netherlands), and groups of employers.

Although subcontracting has the character of a triangular relationship, it is clearly distinguished from temporary employment, which will form the subject of the present section. Subcontracting is confined to the provision of works or services, and it involves the user signing a contract for the performance, for his or her convenience, of a clearly defined task consisting in the provision of works or services. The subcontractor is the sole employer of the employees involved, and they are subject exclusively to the subcontractor's authority.

Temporary employment[36] appears under various forms, and it is

---

36. Temporary employment has been described in a comparative law study as "another way of evading the law and collective agreements"; see Bob Hepple, "Security of Employment", in Blanpain (ed.), *Comparative Labour Law and Industrial Relations*, Kluver, Deventer/ Netherlands, 1982, p. 363.

not treated in the same way by the labour laws of all member countries, although its legal basis in each country is growing stronger. It has not in fact been "legalised" in all member countries. A distinction needs to be drawn straight away between the two forms of temporary employment: temporary employment appearing as (a) staff transfer or worker transfer, where one or more workers are assigned or "lent" by their employer, in exceptional and provisional circumstances, to an outside firm; or (b) staff transfer "improperly so called" according to the German expression, or interim employment in Belgium, where workers are taken on by a temporary employment company for the purpose of being lent out to an outside firm, the "user" firm.

The first manifestation of temporary employment, which is known on the Continent but also in the United Kingdom, is limited in practice,[37] and does not play as large a role as that currently played by temporary employment agencies. This is a relatively new phenomenon; it appeared at the beginning of the 1970s, and it is regulated across the board by legislation which has given it its own charter and which makes it possible for some sort of protection to be given to temporary workers, while still differentiating them clearly from full-time workers. In these cases, companies are subject to strict regulation: these legal systems lay down detailed rules for the triangular relationship existing between the three main protagonists in temporary employment: the temporary employment company, the user company, and the temporary worker. In other countries such as the United Kingdom and Ireland temporary employment, although it does not have its own legal status, has become a dominant force in the labour and recruitment market. Even in countries without any regulation, such as Portugal or the other southern countries where temporary employment is prohibited, one finds agencies and companies which are very highly organised (equipped with computers, for example), whose aim is to supply staff for organising conferences and meetings, or specialist workers for the hotel industry, tourism and comparable services. It is worth noting that in the Grand Duchy of Luxembourg, where temporary employment is also expanding, the Employment Committee, in its plan for the regulation of atypical employment, is also taking an interest in the "temporary subcontracting of sought-after staff".

---

37. This is true, for example, of the United Kingdom where "worker loans" are known but not widely used. It is sometimes practised among white-collar workers (teachers, for example) and skilled workers in certain cases (see P. Leighton, "Forms and Aspects of Atypical Relationships", loc. cit., pp. 313-314). In the Federal Republic of Germany, staff transfer is widespread within groups of companies; in these cases, the company borrowing the workers has, together with the company lending them, some supplementary duties towards the transferred workers.

Regulated and monitored temporary employment: the Federal Republic of Germany, France, Belgium, the Netherlands

● *The Federal Republic of Germany*

Initially prohibited, the activity of temporary employment companies was authorised in 1968, and in 1972 became the subject of a special set of regulations.[38] These were contained in the law on staff hiring (Arbeitnehmerüberlassunggesetz), which regulates on the one hand the relationships between temporary companies and temporary workers, and on the other hand the relationships between the workers and the user companies. After this liberalisation, there was a considerable increase in the numbers of temporary workers in the Federal Republic of Germany.[39] In 1975 there were 9000 temporary workers; by 1982 there were 43,000, without including the (apparently considerable) number of undeclared temporary employees.[40] Some amendments tending to confirm the new liberalisation were contained in the employment promotion law (BeschG) of 1982. The most significant of these is the provision doubling the duration of a placement for a temporary worker:[41] from the passing of this law, until 1 January 1990, a company may use the services of the same temporary employee for a period of six months instead of three.

Under German law temporary employment companies must fulfil certain formal and material conditions. Thus each company must obtain prior authorisation from the labour administration. In principle this authorisation is of a limited duration: it may not exceed a period of one year. But in cases where the company has been in operation for three years, the authorisation may be granted for an indeterminate period. Authorisation may be refused if the company fails to satisfy certain material conditions: non-compliance with employment protection legislation and social security rules, inability to fulfil contractual obligations as an employer, and other factors. In addition, the temporary employment company is liable to be monitored by the

---

38. The breach was opened here by German case-law. A judgement of the Federal Constitutional Court, published in 1968, gave the green light to the legislators: Verf.Ge 21, 261 ff.

39. Däubler, "Crise, maintien de l'emploi", op. cit., p. 29.

40. The book *Ali le Gastarbeiter* makes reference to this category, which also includes foreign workers.

41. This extension, despite its modest appearance and provisional nature, is more significant than one might think; see Bertram Michel, "Federal Republic of Germany". Antoine Lyon-Caen and Antoine Jeammaud, "Droit du travail - démocratie et crise", op. cit., p. 155.

administrative authorities to which it has to provide information on its operations.

The employment promotion law (BeschG) introduces an innovation as regards the authorisation just mentioned; it rules out the granting of such authorisation in a case of hiring within groups of companies whose activity is not based on the transfer of workers, as well as in cases of hiring within the same sector of industry, calculated to avoid partial layoffs and dismissals.

Although the relationship between the temporary employee and the user company does not constitute a real employment relationship, the fact that the temporary worker is performing his or her work in the user company's premises does give the company certain rights and obligations. The worker must respect the work regulations of the user company, which in turn is obliged to extend to the temporary employees all protective provisions[42] laid down by law. The duration of the contract of a temporary employee must be for a maximum of six months. If that period comes to an end and the worker continues to be employed, then a new direct employment relationship comes into being between the temporary employee and the user company. The same applies when the worker is placed in the user company without the required conditions being legally recognised.

The relationship between the temporary worker and the temporary employment company is considered to be a true employment relationship. But to the extent that the temporary employment company is liable to a set of additional obligations, this relationship is not the same as that arising in a typical employment relationship. The employment contract between the temporary employee and the user company must be drawn up in writing and have a specific content which is stipulated in great detail by law. It cannot contain certain clauses which may figure in a traditional employment contract. The employer is not allowed to limit the duration of the temporary contract. This obligation is not, however, obeyed in practice, and the vast majority of temporary employees in the Federal Republic of Germany are bound by a fixed-term contract. The temporary employment company is not entitled to dismiss a temporary worker for economic reasons affecting the user company.

In the Federal Republic of Germany, the temporary worker remains a marginal figure in the user company. Both the pay and the working conditions obtained by temporary employees are less favourable than

---

42. Falkenberg, op. cit., Schaub, Arbeitsrecht, par. 120.IV.2; W. Daubler, Das Arbeitrecht 2, p. 813.

those applying to direct employees of the company, for the following reasons, among others:

(a) temporary workers are excluded from the field of application of collective agreements signed by the user company;

(b) the number of collective agreements signed by temporary employment companies is not large;

(c) temporary workers have no right to vote and to stand for office in the staff representative bodies of the user company, although they do have the right to attend the meetings of some of these bodies;[43]

(d) the social security entitlements of temporary workers are far from guaranteeing them the same rights as workers with a non-precarious employment relationship.

● *France: after hesitating, legislators opt for full recognition*

In France, temporary employment was admitted by legislation in 1972 — the same year as in West Germany — but it was considered initially as a short-lived emergency solution. The unexpected expansion of this type of employment prompted a second legislative intervention in order to restrict the use of temporary employees.[44] In 1985, the range of acceptable cases was enlarged, and in 1986 the limiting list of cases in which recourse to temporary employment would be permissible was abolished.[45] The government, believing that temporary employment and other atypical forms of employment (fixed-term, temporary, part-time) are "precious job deposits whose full exploitation is inhibited by current regulations", removed all obstacles to the use of temporary employees. The temporary employment contract must be drawn up for "the performance of a non-lasting task, except for the replacement of an absent worker, a seasonal job, or a profession in which the use of temporary employment is customary". The law prohibits the use of a temporary employee to perform a normal and permanent activity of the company. The recruitment of temporary staff in cases of industrial dispute is not permitted.

43. Däubler, "Crise, maintien de l'emploi", op. cit.; Daubler, Das Arbeitrecht 2, pp. 813. ff.

44. See J.C. Javillier, French report to the Geneva colloquium, loc. cit., pp. 143 ff.; J. Pelissier, "La relation du travail atypique", French report to the Caracas conference, loc. cit., pp. 528-529.

45. G. Lyon-Caen, "Notes sur quelques nouvelles formes d'emploi et leurs effets en droit du travail et de la sécurité sociale", pp. 8 ff.

The contract between the user company and the temporary employment company (the staff supply contract) must be drawn up in writing, and it must state the reason for recourse to temporary employment, the number of workers required, the skills required, the location, timetable and rates of pay. Even though the contract may contain no clause on the responsibility of the temporary employment company towards the user company as regards possible shortcomings on the part of the temporary employees, there is nevertheless a responsibility, as an agency, for the professional capabilities of the staff supplied.

The contract between the temporary employment company and the temporary worker, the assignment contract, is a fixed-term contract which may be renewed once for the same duration, on condition that the total duration does not exceed 24 months. It must be drawn up in writing and include the clauses and specifications listed in the staff supply contract, the employee's skills or qualifications, the methods of remuneration, etc. The law states that the temporary employee is entitled to:

— a salary at least equal to what would be paid in the user company to an employee with similar qualifications after a trial period occupying the same post;

— payment for free days (independently of seniority) to which employees of the user company are entitled;

— a holiday allowance, paid at the end of the assignment regardless of the duration of the assignment;

— a job insecurity allowance calculated on the basis of the duration of the assignment and the remuneration of the employee — this allowance may not be lower than a minimum level established through a collective agreement or, failing such agreement, by decree.

These provisions, tending to establish equality of treatment, express the wish of legislators to end the disparities in pay which have emerged between permanent company employees and temporary workers, to the detriment of the latter.

There would appear to be no direct legal link between the user company and the temporary worker. In fact, although there is no employment contract binding the temporary employee to the user company, a set of rights and obligations connects them to each other. The user company has authority over the temporary worker, by virtue of the staff supply contract: it is entitled to issue instructions to the temporary employee, who is obliged to carry them out. In return, the user company is subject to a certain number of obligations: it is responsible for the conditions of work performance, as laid down in the standards established by law, regulation and agreement for the workplace; it has the same obligations towards temporary employees as it has towards its own employees in the matter of collective transport facilities and collective installations in general. If the user company continues to make use of a temporary worker after the end of his or her assignment, without having drawn up an employment contract with the temporary worker or a new staff supply contract, the temporary employee is now deemed to be linked to the user by an open-ended contract.

Between two contracts of assignment, the temporary worker is non-existent: he or she is neither unemployed, nor employed, but merely "awaiting a new assignment".[46]

● *Belgium: perpetuating "experimental and provisional" regulations*

The uncontrolled growth of temporary employment companies, a relatively recent phenomenon in Belgium,[47] and the consequent legal and social problems — caused for example by the fact that they lie outside the rules of the social security system — had given rise to lively debate in Belgium before 1976. Two opposing positions emerged: one in favour of prohibiting the activities of temporary employment agencies, and the other in favour of regulating this activity with a view to avoiding abuses and protecting both temporary and permanent workers. Between these opposing positions, Belgian pragmatism devised a compromise solution: provisional regulations.

Thus was born the law of 28 June 1976, valid for four years subject to an extension of one year. After the end of this transitional period, the question of temporary working was to be reviewed. There was a possibility that the functions carried out by the temporary employment companies might be handed over to the National Employment Office, thus causing the companies to cease operations.

However, at the expiry date the dissolution of Parliament prevented the adoption of a new law, and the social partners had to conclude provisional collective agreements (subsequently made compulsory by royal decree) on temporary employment. A recommendation from the National Labour Council (no.771 of 27.11.1981) suggested urgent

---

46. G. Lyon-Caen, French report, p. 11.

47. E. Vogel, Belgian report on "La crise, le maintien de l'emploi et partage du travail", Geneva colloquium, loc. cit., pp. 67 ff; by the same author, *Droit social*, vol. 1: *Les rapports individuels du travail*, PUB, Brussels, 1983-84, pp. 130 ff.; O. Vanachter, M. Vranken, "New forms and aspects of atypical employment relationships", Belgian report to the Caracas conference, loc. cit., pp. 285 ff.

action on temporary employment and the role of the National Employment Office, which can recruit temporary workers and assign them to user companies, while keeping to the rules which govern private temporary employment companies, such as the collective agreements which apply to them. The "eternalisation" of the first version of the rules on temporary employment has been achieved mainly through a collective agreement (no.36) which contains some basic provisions on temporary employment.

The legal regulation of temporary employment is based on the triangular relationship, as in the cases of the Federal Republic of Germany, and France. Temporary employment is permitted only in the following circumstances: (a) replacing a permanent employee; (b) meeting an extraordinary peak in the company's work; (c) ensuring the performance of an exceptional task. The specifications which appear in the contract drawn up between the temporary employment company and the user company must be transmitted in writing to the temporary worker. The temporary employment contract must specify the reason for the contract and its duration, the reason for replacement, the professional qualifications of the temporary employee, the place of work, the timetable, etc. It is illegal to insert clauses prohibiting the conclusion of a contract between the temporary worker and the user company. As a worker's seniority rights are determined by the duration of an uninterrupted employment relationship, which does not apply to a temporary worker, it is considered that the seniority of such a worker is not interrupted: (a) by periods of suspension of the contract during which the worker remains liable for social security; and (b) by periods of inactivity not exceeding one week. A party to the contract who unilaterally cancels the contract prematurely, without a grave reason, is liable to compensate the other party up to the end, through the payment of a specified sum. A temporary employment agency is not allowed to assign temporary workers to a user company, or keep them there, during a strike or lock-out; otherwise the agency runs the risk of having its authorisation suspended.

- *Netherlands: the legal status of the temporary worker is not clearly defined*

The Dutch legal system was one of the earliest to confer a legal status on temporary work: around 1960, temporary workers were brought under the scope of the social security schemes.[48] However, in the

---

48. Antoine Jacobs, Dutch report, op. cit.; Christe Dienand, "New forms and aspects of atypical employment relationships" (Caracas), loc. cit., pp. 6 ff.

full employment situation of the 1960s the activities of "go-betweens" on the labour market caused a lot of unrest, and in 1970 the government decided to forbid temporary work in the construction and engineering industries in the Rotterdam area. As for all other temporary work, the temporary work agencies need a government licence. The conditions for obtaining such a licence force them to offer the same labour conditions to temporary workers as those enjoyed by the fixed staff in the various trades. Moreover placement of a temporary worker in the same enterprise for longer than six months is forbidden.

The trade union movement for a long time was divided in its attitude to temporary work, and only very recently all unions concluded a collective agreement with the temporary work agencies covering all temporary workers (about 100,000). The legal status of the contract of a temporary worker is still not completely clear. On the basis of case law, such a contract, in many cases, has to be regarded as a regular contract of employment between the temporary work agency and the temporary worker, although deviations from this pattern are always possible. Furthermore, it is evident that there is also a certain real relationship between the hiring company and the temporary worker (as regards authority, safety, and the like).

● *United Kingdom: permitted by law, different versions, ill-defined status*

Workers employed under a temporary employment contract and by temporary employment agencies — which burgeoned in the United Kingdom in the 1960s — currently represent about 8% of the total number of employees.[49] Recent studies have shown that there is a structural shift of temporary employees from industry to the tertiary sector. The activities of temporary employment companies are regulated by a 1973 law, the Employment Agencies Act. This, while exercising a certain degree of control[50] over temporary employment companies — it was passed in order to deal with abuses committed by these firms — cannot be compared to the corresponding legislation in the Federal Republic of Germany, in France or in Belgium. The law prescribes official authorisation for "employment businesses" and "employment agencies". These companies must obey some conditions when they supply a temporary worker to an employer: this person must be informed in writing of the recruitment conditions

---

49. NEDO, *Changing Work Patterns*, op. cit., p. 16.

50. See Hepple and O'Higgins, *Employment Law*, 4th edition, London, 1981, pp. 70-71; Paul Davies and M. Freedland, *Labour Law*, op. cit., p. ; P. Leighton, "Forms and aspects", op. cit., pp. 313-314.

and the employment status of people taken on. The temporary worker has a double employment relationship, both with the temporary employment agency (the supplier) and with the user company (the hirer). But the nature of these relationships is not clear in English law. If there is no employment contract between the temporary employee and the user company, then that company may disregard certain rights attaching to the worker, who will then be obliged to take them up with the temporary employment agency. Often, however, that relationship is not governed by an employment contract offering protection to the worker, but by a common-law agreement.

These problems with the status of temporary employees have been emphasised by some authors, who propose the adoption of a "Temporary Working Act"[51] with a view to eliminating them. Case-law, despite a few positive judgements in this area, has not so far managed to define clearly the rights of temporary workers. In fact the courts have come up with surprising findings in the case of Wickens v. Champion Employment, where a temporary employment agency's temporary workers were defined as self-employed.

Spain, Greece, Italy, Portugal:
ban on temporary employment companies, and illegal practices

● *Portugal: old practices and new practices without regulation*

The institution of temporary employment agencies, mainly geared towards the tertiary sector (office-work, accounts), has existed in Portugal for a long time. As Portuguese law does not regulate temporary work, the companies in question have a great deal of discretion in their operations, and no statistics are available on the extent of the phenomenon, although it is by no means negligible, as is generally acknowledged.[52]

In the absence of special provisions, the temporary employment relationship is seen as constituting a simple angular structure made up of two contractual links which are independent of each other from a legal point of view. This is not, then, a "triangular" legal structure; the law does not recognise any legal connection between the worker and the temporary employment company. According to case-law (which is not very copious in this area), the temporary employment

---

51. B.A. Hepple and B.W. Napier, quoted by Davies and Freedland, op. cit., p. 99.

52. Antonio Monteiro Fernandes, "Les relations d'emploi atypique au Portugal", op. cit., p. 3.

company has no responsibility towards the temporary worker.

There are other temporary employment practices in Portugal, which are found mostly in industries undergoing transformation and in the construction industry, where firms provisionally "lend" workers to other firms for payment on either an hourly or a daily basis. This is not, however, a case of staff transfer, because the firms which control the staff are really temporary employment companies which do not recruit workers in order to give them work directly.[53] Recruited under fixed-term contracts, the workers are laid off once the "loan" period has come to an end. If these companies specialising in "recrutemento indirecto" are not envisaged by Portuguese legislation, certain large-scale industrial units are at the centre of temporary worker supply under the guise of subcontracting.

As the vast majority of temporary employees have no contract of employment, and are deprived of all protection, the government introduced a draft law on temporary employment in 1985. Although there has been public debate, the draft law has not made any headway: the communist trade union has taken a stand against recognising temporary employment, while the socialist and social-democratic unions have come out in favour of controlled acceptance.

● *Spain: temporary employment companies are prohibited*

In Spain, article 43.1 of the basic labour law, Statuto de los Trabajadores, repeating an existing stipulation, states clearly that "it is forbidden to recruit or engage workers in order to hire them out or transfer them temporarily to a company".[54] The worker must be recruited directly by the employer; thus the "triangular" relationship does not exist in the Spanish legal system. The law envisages the use of temporary contracts to fill vacant positions in cases where employees are unable to work due to causes such as illness, military service or maternity, and where the duration of the temporary contract depends on how long the contract of the permanent employee being replaced is suspended. Article 15 of the "workers' statute" stipulates that the name of the worker being replaced must be given, and the reason for the suspension of the permanent contract must be stated.

● *Italy and Greece: illegal practices*

Despite prohibitions, one finds the practice of temporary working in both of these countries, especially in tourism, the organisation of

---

53. op. cit., p. 5.

54. See M.A. Olea, "Espagne", Geneva colloquium, loc. cit., pp. 99 ff. See also Federico Durán-Lopez, "Modalidades de contratation laboral", op. cit., passim.

conferences and meetings, and similar activities. In Italy in recent years, some authors have been advancing stern criticisms of the lack of authorisation and regulation of temporary employment businesses in certain sectors: they believe that attention to these could contribute to improved organisation and output.[55]

APPRENTICESHIP CONTRACTS, EMPLOYMENT/TRAINING CONTRACTS

Contracts to promote youth employment

In many countries a version of the fixed-term contract is being combined with apprenticeship and training, to produce a new category of contracts designed for young people: mostly, these are employment and training contracts. Apprenticeship and job experience contracts were already known in all countries, but it is well known that their role up to recently has been a limited one.

The new forms of work for young people are designed to facilitate their entry into the labour market at a time when, in all countries, the very high unemployment rate and the lack of hope for a sharp improvement in the employment level are creating a dramatic situation. The state, through this new legislation, is encouraging companies to take on a certain percentage of young people, by offering certain incentives which vary from country to country. They can take the form of governments meeting young people's social security obligations, or paying part of their salaries, or even providing tax breaks. While state action shows the tendency (and concern) of modern labour law to protect companies through this type of assistance, the employment/training contract also reflects the new requirements of work organisation in companies in what is called "post-industrial" society.

France

In France, two new types of employment contract connected with the entry of young people into employment have been added to the traditional work experience "stage", designed to initiate young people to the world of work, and the apprenticeship contract. The new contracts are the qualification contract and the adaptation contract for young people aged between 16 and 25.

The qualification contract's aim is to allow young people to gain

---

55. T. Treu, quoted by Hepple in *Security of Employment*, loc. cit.

a recognised professional qualification, or one in the course of recognition, within the classification of sectoral collective agreement. It involves a dual training, in other words, theoretical training and on-the-job training. Only employers officially certified by the public authorities may propose qualification contracts. This certification is subject either to the company concluding an agreement with a public teaching institution or training body, or to the company joining in a framework agreement drawn up between the state and a professional organisation. The duration of the qualification contract, which must be drawn up in writing and registered with the departmental labour directorate, is for a minimum of six months and a maximum of two years. General teaching provided during the period of the contract must represent at least 25% of the total duration of the contract.

The adaptation contract is a real employment contract which aims to offer young people training which is complementary to a previously acquired qualification. The adaptation contract, which provides for a process of adaptation to the job, alternating with theoretical training, may be either a fixed-term contract of at least six months, or else an open-ended contract. The worker is entitled to remuneration equivalent to at least 80% of the minimum salary specified by the collective agreement which applies to the company; in any case, the salary cannot be lower than the SMIC (statutory minimum wage).

Workers on a qualification contract or an adaptation contract are not counted in the staff totals for the company. The recruitment of a young person under an adaptation or qualification contract exempts the employer from all contributions for social security, occupational accidents and family allowances.

Italy

The employment/training contract (contratto di formazione e lavoro) introduced into the Italian legal system by law no.285 of 1977 in order to stimulate youth employment, and reinforced by law no.863 of 1984, may be drawn up with young people aged between 15 and 29. The duration of this type of contract must not exceed 24 months, and it cannot be renewed. The only type of company entitled to draw up employment/training contracts is one which has prepared plans relating and corresponding to regional or national regulations on vocational training. These plans must describe precisely the kind of training that the worker will receive and the kind of work that he or she will carry out. They have to be submitted to the regional employment committee (commissione regionale per l'impiego), which is made up of representatives of the state, the region and the trade union organisations. The committee has to pronounce on the ability of the submitted plans to fulfil the function of this category of contracts, i.e. training. In some cases, however, where these training plans are prepared according to rules established by the collective agreement, approval from the regional employment committee is not required. Moreover, the law states that training plans drawn up by common agreement between employers and trade unions have a prior call on financing in relation to other plans.

Spain

In Spain a new law, decree no.1992 of 31 October 1984, has taken charge both of training contracts and work experience contracts, favouring these "new" forms and encouraging the conclusion of contracts in this category.

As regards the agreement of training contracts, the age limit of workers eligible for recruitment under these contracts has been changed: the age-group envisaged is young people aged between 16 and 20. The duration of the training contract may be for a minimum of three months and a maximum of three years. The proportion of time used for the training of workers may not be lower than a quarter, nor higher than half of the total time. The wages paid to a worker under a training contract are proportional to the actual duration of the work done.

The work experience contract can be drawn up after the end of the worker's studies, and during a period of four years. The duration of the contract can be for a minimum of three months and a maximum of three years. A work experience contract may be renewed several times. In this case too, the wage paid to a worker under a work experience contract is proportional to the real time of the work done, as in the case of a training contract.

In the case of both the training contract and the work experience contract, the social security contributions normally payable by the employer are drastically reduced. For work experience contracts the reduction is 75%, while for training contracts the employer is totally exempt from the normal obligations if the company employs fewer than twenty people; otherwise the employer benefits from a 90% reduction.

Portugal

In Portugal, one also finds an increase in the number of work experience contracts in recent years. In one category of work experience contracts schools are involved: certain private high schools which have links — sometimes quite close links — with business. This is also true of some middle-level technical schools. In this latter case, the law (order no.253/84) calls for the establishment of work experience agreements between the school and the company governing the relationship between the participating worker, the school, and the company.

The enormous number of work experience contracts merely reflects direct agreements between the young worker and the company. A work experience contract does not have the same status as an apprenticeship contract, and thus it manages to avoid the controls prescribed by the relevant law (order no.102/84); it is also different from an employment contract. In fact, this type of contract stipulates such a large proportion of work obligations, in relation to the clauses covering teaching and training duties, that its main function is obviously as a fixed-term contract of employment stripped of the protection which Portuguese law extends to this category of employment contracts.

Belgium

In Belgium, alongside the existing work experience schemes and contracts, a new employment/training contract has been introduced by a royal decree published during January 1987 (article 495, *Moniteur belge*, 23 January 1987), which envisages a system "combining work and training for young people aged between 18 and 25, and allowing a temporary reduction in employers' social security contributions payable in respect of these young people". The employer must draw up a "work-training" agreement with the young worker. This stipulates that the employer is taking on the worker under the terms of a fixed-term contract including work and training. The minimum duration of this agreement is one year, and the maximum is three years. The employer benefits from a reduction in the employer's social security contributions, in proportion to the work duties prescribed.

Labour law texts dealing with youth employment are proliferating at the moment in Belgium. Another royal decree, published on the same day, allows for temporary reductions in employers' social security contributions to encourage the employment of young people and the long-term unemployed, while a third decree, promulgated a few days before the other two, raises the age-limit for a worker on an apprenticeship contract of the so-called industrial kind from 18 to 21 years.

HYBRID AND INNOVATIVE FORMS:
KAPOVAZ AND INTERMITTENT WORKING

There are also forms of employment which are effectively new, innovative and, one might say, unclassifiable because they are hybrid. These forms are developing in all countries, especially those at the centre of the Community. Labour law, which is still puzzled by these novelties, is beginning to tackle them: in the Federal Republic of Germany the law on job protection is tackling the "KAPOVAZ" system, while in the Netherlands case-law is beginning to deal with "on-call" working.

Regulation of flexible working: KAPOVAZ

Although new regulations on employment, based on the logic of flexibility and the requirements of economic units which control workers, are constantly emerging in companies in all countries, we find on the other hand that there are very few legislative texts which regulate flexible working in the strict sense. German legislators have made an effort. In the employment promotion law (BeschFG),[56] they deal with those work timetables which vary according to the needs of the company (Kapazitätsorientierte variable Arbeitszeit: "KAPOVAZ"), which have been causing various problems for the workers.[57] In effect, uncertainty about working time compels these workers to be permanently at their employers' beck and call, which prevents them from organising their free time (protection of the worker's personal lifestyle), and also prevents them from possibly entering into another part-time employment contract with a view to earning an income large enough for their needs.

In cases where a worker has to provide services in accordance with the amount of work to be done at any one time, under "KAPOVAZ", article 3 of the BeschFG lays down three conditions: (a) the work contract must specify the duration of working, so this is not "work on call";[58] (b) the employee is obliged to work only when he or she

---

56. W. Däubler, "Crise, maintien de l'emploi, partage du travail", op. cit.

57. Hoyningen-Huene, "Rechtliche Gestaltungsmöglichkeiten beim Job-sharing Arbeitsverhältänis", *Betriebs-Berater*, 1982, p. 1240.

58. The contract must fix "the duration", but it is not entirely clear whether this is the weekly, monthly or yearly duration. The legal literature is divided, and the BAG has not yet pronounced upon the question. If no duration of working is stipulated, it is assumed that a duration of 10 hours per week has been agreed (article 1 paragraph 4 subsection 1).

has been notified four days in advance. Failing this, the employee is not obliged to perform work duties, unless he or she is willing to do so — and wishes at the same time to keep his or her job; (c) the worker cannot be called in for very short periods of work: each work assignment must be for at least three consecutive hours.

2. "Labour on call": some problems

Work "on call" or "on demand" is another form of atypical work which creates a tangle of legal problems. The potential worker is available to the employer, who may call the worker at any moment. This type of work, which is not much liked by the trade unions, is spreading in some sectors of industry, commerce, services, air transport, hotels and tourism.

One of the specific problems faced by this category of workers is that of waiting without being called, or being called too infrequently to work. What about this waiting period, which can be excessively long? Should the worker receive a "minimum remuneration" on the grounds that he or she is at the employer's disposal? Can any relationship be envisaged with the unemployment allowance system? On what conditions? Labour on call is treated in different ways from one country to the next. In the Netherlands,[59] employers have developed a wide range of labour-on-call contracts: one of them is the so-called min-max-contract, in which the employer guarantees a minimum and a maximum of work to the worker.

Judges also discern various types of labour-on call-contracts. In one type it is assumed that the worker has placed him/herself at the employer's disposal by a kind of pre-contract; a contract of employment in the strict sense only exists during the periods in which the worker effectively performs work. In a second type, the existence of a contract of employment is assumed right from the start, even if the obligations to provide and to perform work are considered to be postponed and interrupted from time to time. It is clear that the first category offers less protection to the worker.

In case law, judges tend to prefer the allocation of labour-on-call contracts to the second type as soon as they suspect abuses. In case law a certain right of the worker to be effectively provided with work is recognised, but so conditionally as to make it virtually impossible to invoke it. Labour-on-call is barely regulated by collective agreements; statutory law lacks any specific provision on this matter,

---

59. Antoine Jacobs, Dutch report, loc. cit.; Christe Dienand, "New forms and aspects of atypical employment relationship", Dutch report to the Caracas conference, loc. cit., pp. 28 ff.

although a committee of government officials is at the moment considering legislation in this field.

The existence of this contract for labour on call does not resolve the problems of the waiting period, nor those arising from employment on such a short timetable that it does not allow the "on call" workers to benefit from the minimum levels set by labour law and the social security system.

HOME-BASED WORK AND TELEWORKING, "FLOATING FORMS": THE CRITERION OF SUBORDINATION MAY DISAPPEAR

INTRODUCTION: TWO DISTINCT FORMS OF WORK SHARING COMMON FEATURES

Home-based work and teleworking are two new forms of work, but the first of these is really very old; it was well known in the last century, and was subjected to legal regulation. That is not the case with teleworking, which is a genuinely new form of work. It is anticipated that teleworking will have a major and pervasive role in the future, and it is raising new problems for lawyers which have yet to be resolved. Although they have some points in common, these two forms of atypical employment are not the same. In fact, it is necessary to distinguish them clearly one from the other, but there are common features shared by these two atypical forms: the workplace which is not located in the company, and the peculiar nature of the employer-employee relationship.

In the typical subordinate employment relationship, one of the classic and essential elements is the fact that work duties are performed in the company's premises: one finds unity of place and work. Home-based work has long been an exception to this general rule. The same is true of teleworking which basically provokes, or rather exposes, the spatial explosion of the workplace which is inherent in the development of technology. Distance from the workplace gives the employer-employee relationship in these cases some peculiar features.

HOME-BASED WORK: REAPPEARING IN STRENGTH, WITHOUT BEING TIED TO NEW TECHNOLOGY

This very old form of work was, at the end of the nineteenth century, linked to the achievements of new technology at the time, such as the appearance of very light, cheap sewing-machines which could be used at home, instead of the bulky, powerful sewing-machines which had dictated that workers must be concentrated together in one spot.[60] It is now reappearing in all countries, indeed in quite a powerful way.[61]

In all member states, home-based work had already been legally regulated, even if this regulation was only a rudimentary one, as in the case of Greece. The problem of this category of workers who, by virtue of their working conditions in the home, are very close to self-employed workers — isolation from the company, no employer supervision in carrying out work duties, self-determination of the duration of timetables and working time — has always been to mark themselves off from the self-employed and join the system of employed labour. As it went through something of a decline during the years of economic prosperity, this form of work was somewhat "neglected" by labour law, but now that it is in its "revival" phase, gaining importance and extending to intellectual work (e.g. translators, draughtsmen), it is posing new legal problems.

The Federal Republic of Germany

In the Federal Republic of Germany, home-based work is governed by the "Heimarbeitsgesetz" (HAG) of 1951, which gives home-based workers the same status as employed workers. A home-based worker is defined as somebody who, at the request of an employer, performs, at home or in premises of his or her own choice, paid work of an industrial nature — connected with the manufacture, processing or packing of merchandise — the products of which are directly or indirectly exploited by the employer. A home-based tradesman, employing up to a maximum of two helpers, is subject to the same legal system. Apart from the extension of protection deriving from the law and from collective agreements applicable to company employees and home-based workers, the law also stipulates that home-based work must be subject to administrative controls.

Belgium

In Belgium, despite the fact that home-based work was regulated by law as early as 1934, it is currently without any general provisions

---

60. A. Erazy, "Les impacts des technologies sur la vie au travail", in R. Dury (ed.), *Femmes et nouvelles technologies*, op. cit., p. 40.

61. See Lipsig Mumme, "La renaissance du travail à domicile dans les économies développées", *Sociologie du Travail*, number 3/83, pp. 313 ff.

regulating it as such. The legal position of the home-based worker is thus rather ambiguous.[62] For a long time, the legal literature and case-law had set a clear boundary between a manual worker's contract and a home work contract, based on the criterion relating to the concept of subordination. The 1978 law on employment contracts, which replaces the 1900 law, does not include the home-based contract within its field of application, on the basis, among other things (as the reasoning states), that "home-based workers choose their own place of work". In short, the main stumbling-block against applying labour law to home-based workers in Belgium was the concept of subordination of the employee to the employer's requirements. There is also a gap in the relevant legislation, to the extent that the provisions relating to home-based working were abrogated, without anything being put in their place.

According to a portion of the legal literature, which takes account of the case-law tending towards a more flexible interpretation of the conditions involved in the concept of subordination, it could be held that "legislation on employment contracts has now become applicable to home-based workers" who are manual workers and employed.[63] Even if this interpretation were universally accepted, which is not the case, there would be a need for changes in the legislation covering home-based working in an overall approach. The ambiguity of the legal status of these workers, the partial and sporadic character of other texts dealing with home-based working, the fact that there are no joint committees for home-based workers, and the fact that collective agreements drawn up within the National Council are not automatically applied to home-based workers,[64] are all reasons for urging this reform.

Spain

The regulation of home-based working is a recent phenomenon in Spain, being covered in the 1980 Statuto de los Trabajadores. According to the provisions of this workers' charter, home-based working is considered as subordinate working. The contract must be in writing, and it must stipulate the place of work. In this way, the labour inspectorate is able to check whether measures concerned with

---

62. Eliane Vogel-Polsky, "Rapport sur les nouvelles formes", op. cit., p. 15.

63. See Supreme Court judgement, 26 September 1973: "....authority is not ruled out by the fact that the worker is carrying out his or her work in a place which is not designated by the employer"; see details and developments in Eliane Vogel-Polsky, op. cit., pp. 79 ff.

64. Op. cit., p. 31.

health and safety are being observed. Home-based workers are entitled to a salary at least equal to what an employee in the same professional category would receive. They also have a right to collective representation. In addition, the workers are entitled to information on processes, salaries and goods connected with their work; the law obliges the employer to give them a document relating to these questions.

Despite all this, there are many home-based workers in Spain who work in the black economy.

Italy

In Italy,[65] home-based working was first regulated by law no.2640 of 1958, and later by law no.877 of 1973, which contains a broader concept of subordination for this type of contract in relation to the traditional employment contract. The home-based worker carries out his or her work at home, possibly with the assistance of family members, on behalf of one or more employers, using materials supplied by the employer. The worker is obliged to comply with the employer's directives relating to the performance of the work, etc.

An employer intending to employ home-based workers must register on an official list; home-based working is thus subject to administrative controls. The worker receives the rates of payment laid down in the collective agreement for the category of workers with which he or she has parity. In cases where there is no such agreement, rates of pay are fixed by a regional joint commission. Debates are continuing on the protection of home-based workers, who do not always enjoy the same protection as company-based workers.[66] From the point of view of social security, the home-based worker has the same rights as the company-based worker, with one exception: he or she is excluded from the industrial sector's "cassa integrazione guadagni" (wages supplement fund), which means the loss of very significant amounts of compensation if work is suspended or reduced.

Loaded with the mitigated protection afforded by labour law, which is concerned to avoid classifying home-based working — a kind of subordinate employment — pseudo-independent and pseudo-craft work flourish in Italy. However, in this country we also find, as we

---

65. Bruno Veneziani, National report, pp. 10 ff.; Franco Carinci, "Las nuevas formas y aspectos de la relacion del trabajo atipica", Italian report to the Caracas conference, loc. cit., pp. 100 ff.; Edoardo Ghera, *Diritto del lavoro*, op. cit.

66. The Italian supreme court judgement of 17.3.81 should be borne in mind: it considers that the individual dismissal system is applicable to home-based working where there is evidence of "qualified continuity" of work by the home-based worker.

have seen, this new concept of subordination: the home-based worker, even when assisted by family members, using materials belonging to the worker or to the employer, is considered as a subordinate employee, "on the grounds that he or she is obliged to comply with directives covering methods of manufacture, features and qualities of work to be done whether in the partial manufacture, the finishing, or the total production of the products with which the worker's activity is concerned". Thus we find a debate, inspired broadly by the development of this category of atypical workers, on the redefinition of the field of application for labour law.

United Kingdom

In the United Kingdom one also finds the re-emergence of the category of workers known since the last century by the name of "outworkers". The extent of this phenomenon was realised after a study of poverty carried out in 1968. The number of "homeworkers" continues to increase dramatically. Workers who work "at or from home" are now believed to number well over half a million.[67] No clear definition of the homeworker can be found in English law, and the legal status of these people is by no means clear. Recent studies, which have pointed out the bad working conditions, isolation and low pay of these workers, have also emphasised the lack of legal protection which characterises a large number of them, and offer proposals to remedy this situation.[68] Although the unions have had an opportunity to decide, and to categorise home-based workers as "employees", which means that they are an integral part of the company's production process, with the right to be counted among the company staff and to enjoy protection (against dismissal, for instance) and receive the same pay and other advantages as the company-based employees, they have refused to make any statement on the general position of this category of workers.

The legal literature, while emphasising the absence of a charter or legal protection, and the inadequacy of the responses provided by case law, proposes the adoption of legislative measures which would prescribe among other things — copying continental legislation in this regard — the registration of homeworkers. A Homeworkers' Charter,

---

67. See Patricia Leighton, loc. cit., p. 316; W. Wedderburn, op. cit., p. 130; Paul Davies and Mark Freedland, *Labour Law ...*, op. cit., p. 103; and especially for recent data Catherine Hakim, "Homeworking in Britain", *Employment Gazette*, February 1987.

68. See Paul Davies and Mark Freedland, op. cit., pp. 103 ff.; W. Wedderburn, op. cit., pp. 130 ff. and the bibliography given.

adopted at a national conference in 1985, demands that all home-based workers should have the status of employees, with guaranteed minimum wage levels, and social security rights. The trade unions are trying to attract this category of workers into their ranks, stressing that a lack of representation is no help in defending their interests.

In the meantime, homeworking is continuing to expand, and the stereotype of the worker at home, or from home, continues to change and grow more complex.

Netherlands

In the Netherlands,[69] the position of home-workers was first regulated by an Act of 1933 which largely remained a dead letter. Projects in the 1950s to update this legislation were shelved. In the few cases examined in court, judges tended to consider home-workers' contracts as genuine contracts of employment. Under social security schemes home-workers are in theory treated like other workers, but in most cases they are effectively excluded by an exception for workers earning less than 2/5 of the minimum wage. The Labour Inspectorate has difficulty controlling the working conditions of home-workers, and collective agreements still largely disregard them.[70]

Parliament picked up the issue in 1982, but very recently the government rejected all proposals to improve the lot of home-workers by new statutory provisions.

Portugal

The legal status of home-based working in Portugal is very ill-defined. While the law assumes that there must be a relationship of economic dependency between the worker and the person who is going to receive the fruits of the work if home-based working is to be considered as a form of subordinate work, it does not define the content of that economic dependency. The criteria adopted by the legal literature and case-law are not always very clear. Moreover, the 1969 law on employment contracts, which decided to treat home-

---

69. See Christine Dienand, ''New forms and aspects of atypical employment relationships'', Dutch report to the Caracas conference, vol. II, pp. 26 ff.

70. The enquiry also revealed the psychological condition of home-based workers, whose situation prevents them from using their skills to insist on better rates of payment, for fear of dismissal; this is the slave-labour side of this work which, according to the authors of the report, interferes with the quality of their social life. Vronwenbond FNV, *Thuiswerk, voor fou tien anderen*, Amsterdam, 1981; and Dienand, loc. cit.

working contracts in the same way as a regular employment contract, so that the same principles could be applied, has not succeeded in that objective. In fact, this law states that contracts which have been given parity with regular employment contracts will be subject to special regulations. At the time of writing (Spring 1987), this had not yet happened. By virtue of this, the prevailing interpretation is that the 1969 law does not apply to home-based working. Thus, home-based working is still in a legislative vacuum, except as regards questions relating to occupational accidents and diseases.

Greece

In Greece, home-based working comes under the legal conditions of salaried employment in cases where it is characterised as such, as a form of subordinate work. The 1953 law which contains this provision, without extending to other aspects of home-based working, introduces one exception: home-based workers in a subordinate position in small towns with a population of under 6000 are not entitled to equal pay with salaried workers, nor to Sunday rest, etc. In cases where home-based working is not qualified as subordinate employment, it is considered as self-employment and does not come under the rules of labour law. In such cases, workers are without contracts of service.

Home-based working by women on behalf of industry — making garments, shoes, etc. — has shown a considerable increase in recent years, especially in Athens and Salonika. There are small firms who sack their workers and then give them work to do at home. In such cases the workers lose their standing as employees, take on the status of self-employed, and are paid on a piecework basis. There are firms which do not even have premises and work exclusively with home-based workers, giving them work regularly. The number of so-called "made-to-measure" workers is between 150,000 and 200,000 people according to the Labour Ministry, but even higher according to trade union estimates. In the services sectors too, home-based working is taking on new dimensions (typing, translation, caring). As the vast majority of these workers — who are women — have self-employed status, the question of minimum protection arises urgently.

Denmark

There are always exceptions. In Denmark, home-based working has not developed, and is still undeveloped today, although it is frequently discussed, as is teleworking.[71] If an employer bound by a collective agreement — the classic legal method for regulating employment relationships in this country — attempts to introduce home-based working without the consent of the trade union side of the agreement, this constitutes a violation of the collective agreement which is supposed to cover work done in the workplace provided by the employer.

INCOMPLETE LEGAL STATUS; SLIDE TOWARDS SELF-EMPLOYED STATUS

The shared problems common to home-based workers in all member states (leaving aside the low pay which they receive), arise from their unclear and incomplete legal status. The duration of work, health and safety conditions, questions of professional training, the exercise of collective rights, conditions governing dismissal and protection against unemployment — these issues have hardly ever been raised for this category of isolated workers, who are anyway often marked by a small-time self-employed mentality. Their most immediate problem lies in the precariousness of their situation and their slide, in practical terms, towards the condition of self-employment: the home-based worker who is treated the same as the company-based worker, even when the law grants this worker a lesser degree of legal protection, still costs the employer dear (social security costs, tax burdens, etc.). If for a certain period the employer gives no work to the company's home-based workers, they become self-employed workers with no customers: now, these workers who are without any capital may start working again on exactly the same conditions of effective subordination and economic dependency for the same company — hitherto their employer and henceforth their customer — since they have acquired the status of independent workers. The reality is that they join the swelling ranks of the category of fictitious self-employment, known in Italy as ''para-subordinate'' workers, which the labour and social security law can no longer ignore.

It should also be pointed out that the legal problems posed by intellectual work in the home, apart from telework — translation, teaching, etc — are not taken into consideration by the rules in force in the majority of member states.

---

71. Ruth Nielsen, Paper on the impact of new forms of work and activities on labour law and social security law.

TELEWORK: MOVING INTO ALL AREAS, IT HAS NOT YET BEEN ADDRESSED BY SPECIFIC REGULATIONS

Telework, the newest form of work organisation, appeared during the 1960s, being inherent in the development of new technology,[72] espcially telematics, the technology which brings together computers and telecommunications. Telework is an activity which "necessitates the use of office procedures[73] organised through the means of telecommunications". Now, this type of work organisation allows work to be carried out at a distance: the work can be performed by workers who are in a place far from the employer (or the company) that employs them. Telework can be done either in a separate establishment belonging to the company — the "tele-workplace", which applies to one category of workers employed in banking and insurance — or else in the home. It is on this axis that telework joins up with home-based working. In such cases these two forms of work may share a series of common problems created by the long line of command, or the isolation of home-based workers, with consequences at various levels.

Certain very optimistic forecasts on the extension of telework have given rise to a copious literature on this atypical form, although the actual number of workers involved is, for the moment, extremely limited.[74]

---

72. G. Braun, "Le télétravail", *Droit social*, July-August 1981, pp. 569 ff. See R. Lemesle, "Le télétravail: contribution à l'élaboration de dispositions internes et de normes internationales spécifiques de droit du travail", thesis for the University of Paris/Dauphine (1984), summarised in *Bulletin d'information sociale* (BIS) no.3-4/1984, pp. 441 ff.; G. Metayer, "Télétravail: une alternative", *Autrement*, dossier no.37, February 1982; Eliane Vogel (report), pp. 5 ff.; and also *Télétravail: impact sur les conditions de vie et de travail*, published by the European Foundation for the Improvement of Living and Working Conditions, Dublin, 1984.

73. See R. Lemesle, op. cit.; see also "Empirica Telework: attitudes of the social partners and the labour force and the properties for decentralised work in Europe", in the proceedings of the colloquium organised by the European Foundation in Brussels on 25 April 1986, pp. 91-95; Slavenca Peles, "Les questions juridiques posées en Belgique par le télétravail à domicile", *Travail et Société*, 1986, pp. 87 ff.; Elsbeth Monod, "Le télétravail ou l'arbre qui cache la forêt", *Les Temps Modernes*, no.447, October 1983, pp. 671 ff.

74. The association of the idea that home-based working is an atypical form which mainly concerns women — it allows them to perform their domestic tasks, bring up young children, etc. — and that telework, by invading workers' living-space, will mostly involve women workers, has also given rise to studies, colloquia and research projects on women and new technology. See, for example, Raymonde Dury (ed.), *Femmes et nouvelles technologies*, Labor, Brussels, 1986; G. Doniol-Shaw, "Les femmes dans l'industrie et les changements technologiques", in *Pénélope*, special "Femmes et Techniques" number, October 1983; Christine Jonckheere, Margaretha Lisein-Norman, Monique Chalude, "Analyse des formations aux nouvelles technologies de l'information en vue de prévenir les difficultés d'emploi et certains groupes de travailleurs particulièrement vulnérables: les travailleurs féminins", study carried out for the EEC under the direction of Eliane Vogel-Polsky, May 1984.

Telework, or at any rate the phenomenon of "teleworkers", bursting the spatial boundaries of the workplace and characterised by a very high degree of intensity, is already raising a series of new legal problems in those countries where it is used systematically: Italy, for example, Germany, Belgium or the United Kingdom. In other countries, such as the Netherlands, Denmark, Greece and Portugal, this form of employment has not yet assumed enough significance to provoke a specific legal debate. So far, at all events, no member country has evolved specific regulations for telework. It has been thought sufficient to apply the rules governing either a typical or an atypical employment relationship, depending on circumstances. As a general rule, telework is considered as a form of subordinate employment which may be governed by a traditional employment contract or an atypical employment contract, including a home-worker's contract.[75] Thus, in the Federal Republic of Germany, the very recent phenomenon of telework has not been accorded its own specific set of regulations; in cases where it does not come under an atypical employment contract, and where home-based working is involved, telework is governed by the special laws on home-based workers. Thus, despite its character as non-manual work ("Angestellten Arbeit"), telework falls into the field of application of the 1951 "Heimarbeitsgesetz" (law on home-based working). This law, through its second paragraph, in fact affords equal protection to all other forms of paid home-based work, independently of whether this work is manual, craft-based or otherwise. It should be noted, in this connection, that the German trade unions have proposed that telework should be designated, by a special provision, as a form of subordinate employment, and that teleworkers should be guaranteed access to all trade union rights, including the right to participate in the general assembly of the company, the right to meet union representatives, and other rights.[76/77]

In Belgium, home-based teleworking comes under the laws

---

75. In Denmark, also, a project suggested by the postal service was abandoned, because among other things it had met with opposition from the Danish trade unions (report by E. Vogel, p. 9). As A. Monteiro Fernandes observes in his report, while the problem of legal classification arises in these countries too, it must be recognised that home-based working will be the only one which can be used, burdened with its own problems according to which country is involved.

76. See Däubler in "Pontignano 3", loc. cit.

77. Fearing isolation, lack of social protection, absence of trade union solidarity and disturbances in women's family life, the women members of the SPD, supported by various independent German women's groups, have envisaged a ban on working on a VDU at home. See *Femmes d'Europe*, no.39, January-March 1985, p. 12.

governing home-based working which, as we have seen, are characterised by ambiguity and a fragmentary nature.[78]

In the United Kingdom — where telework seems to employ a greater number of workers than elsewhere, while still remaining limited despite its potential — teleworkers have the same legal status as "homeworkers", which is quite confused, as we have seen. The consequence of this is that very often they receive less pay than workers on the company staff, or else they work on an occasional basis and suffer all the drawbacks which go with their unprotected status as "second-class citizens".[79]

SPECIAL REGULATIONS

Extending the legal status of the home-based worker to cover the teleworker does not seem to offer a solution to the specific problems posed by telework, especially as in the majority of member countries the legal status of home-based working is concerned with manual work, which is itself often outdated. What is needed instead — although this depends on the legal context in each state — is that special regulations should work through agreements[80] or legislation in two directions:

(a) the treatment of the teleworker in the same way as the company-based worker;

(b) the adaptation of labour law rules relating, for example, to worker protection or the exercise of collective worker rights, to the specifics of this form of work.

It is important to have the same rights as workers employed in a company as regards, inter alia, Sunday or weekend rest time, the duration of work, and openings for promotion. As new technology allows a reinforcement of the structures of authority[81] and the

---

78. On the current status of teleworkers in Belgian law, and the measures to be taken in order to secure effective protection, see the detailed and far-reaching research project directed by Eliane Vogel. loc. cit.

79. See U. Huws, "The new technology homeworkers", *Employment Gazette*, 1984, pp. 92 ff.; W. Wedderburn, *Workers and the Law*, op. cit., p. 130; P. Leighton, loc. cit., p. 317.

80. To deal with the problems posed by home-based telework, the confederation of European trade unions, at its European conference in May 1983, stated in its summary report that if telework were to develop " ... it would be high time that on a union level, at least on the basis of negotiations, collective agreements would guarantee the rights of women and men obliged to do this kind of work".

81. See N. Delruelle-Vosszinkel in Raymonde Dury (ed.), *Femmes et nouvelles technologies*, op. cit., pp. 19 ff.

centralisation and/or intensification of the control exercised by the employer, it follows that the employer will have to be made amenable to some rules relating to the protection of basic worker rights. One problem is the protection of workers in relation to the automatic processing of personal data. National debates also indicate a need for appropriate health and safety measures for teleworkers, such as the testing of eyesight and the testing of ergonomic criteria for teleworkers using cathode ray video screens, and also for preventive measures against isolation which can cause nervous disorders.

Other issues are the treatment of teleworkers on the same basis of company workers as regards the exercise of their collective rights, such as being counted in staff totals, and the right to be elected to company bodies and so participate in decision-making, given also that new technology allows decisions to be taken at an earlier stage.[82]

It should be pointed out that the trade union organisations in member states are proposing that teleworkers should have the status of subordinate employees, and a written contract which — for monitoring purposes — should be communicated both to the representative organs of the company and to the labour inspectorate.

EMPLOYMENT WITHOUT AN EMPLOYER

Under this title one must recall the modern procedures for externalising the workforce, such as the shift to subsidiary firms, which has become a procedure for externalising the workforce through structural organisation, or subcontracting in the true sense; these procedures may have the effect of concealing the employer. Subcontracting is certainly not a new legal phenomenon — nor are black-market work and clandestine employment. These are forms of employment which have been known for a very long time, whether or not they evade the controls of labour law. What gives them a genuinely new dimension is, once again, their size and shape.

MODERN TECHNIQUES FOR HIDING THE EMPLOYER

A traditional example of "employment without an employer" would be a home-based worker with the status of a self-employed person while really working as an employee. But employer concealment has

82. See below, paragraph on "collective rights".

taken on more complicated and widespread forms in our day. Staff externalisation, with the advantages which it brings to the real employer, is practised in big firms — including multinationals — through the decentralisation of their management. Restructuring followed by a shift to subsidiary firms, much used over the past ten years, makes it possible for the parent company to carry out a task which was formerly integrated within the company, through a subsidiary firm controlled by the parent company but having its own legal identity.[83] The employment problems arising in groups of companies, also involving new forms of employment, have been studied at Community level, we know, within the works on the proposed Vredeling directives. Other procedures allowing the externalisation of the workforce and/or a type of employer concealment, and which are practised by the big firms in all member states, are service contracts and subcontracting. Here, as we have seen, a company makes an agreement for another company to carry out all or part of a production or service assignment which it is supposed to carry out itself.

THE NEW SELF-EMPLOYED

The constant rise in the number of self-employed workers reflects the current trend, in all countries, towards the transformation of salaried employees into self-employed workers. The percentage of positions transformed in this way is not to be added onto the total of traditional self-employed activities on an equal footing. The fact is that in the overwhelming majority of cases these are fake self-employed people, who continue working for the same employer as previously, under the same conditions of economic dependency: thus one finds a large number of unskilled manual workers swelling the ranks of the ''self-employed''. These are often close to the marginal strata of society. There is also a close correlation between certain forms of sub-contracting, self-employed work, and employment in the black economy. The shift from fake self-employment to black-market employment is often very easy. More and more frequently one finds, among the self-employed, one-person companies which are sometimes engaged in a subcontracting situation.

What is equally relevant to note, in the context of the general observation that current labour law is tending to reinvent the age-old trend towards treating a certain number of low-paid self-employed

---

83. G. Lyon-Caen, ''Plasticité de l'emploi et nouvelles formes d'emploi'', loc. cit., p. 13.

in the same way as salaried employees, is the attitude being taken by case-law, in certain member states, whereby wage-earners working in traditional subordinate positions are treated as self-employed. One finds some classic cases in the United Kingdom,[84] such as the case of the ''self-employed'' waiter who ''rents'' the tables and chairs every day at the establishment where he works. In the Netherlands lorry drivers, who are hired together with their vans by transport companies, are considered as ''self-employed'' (even though the law has forbidden such interpretations). The problem with this new category of self-employed — the category of fake self-employed — lies in those areas of subordination which are less blatantly ''visible'' than in the case of café workers or lorry drivers.

PROBLEMS OF SUBCONTRACTING

The phenomenon of subcontracting (see below, 2.4.4) is no longer confined to some traditional sectors, such as the building industry, as was previously the case. The break-up of big business has been facilitated by the appearance of the phenomenon of ''internal'' subcontracting, whereby a company has another company carry out, on its own premises, one or more functions necessitated by its activities.

Often, this is simply a workforce supply operation, which may, in some countries such as France, constitute the crime of ''marchandage'' (illegal subcontracting). This has harmful effects on workers and labour law — indeed, the same is true of genuine subcontracting. It favours pressure for wage cuts, non-compliance with agreements, and the distortion of obligations arising from legislation on dismissals; also, it hinders the exercise of trade union rights.

Most member states have no special regulations on subcontracting work, with the exception of Belgium where a royal decree of 1978 compels subcontracting companies to register and to deposit a sum of money as a guarantee against possible debts. The law does not provide any special rules for workers employed by subcontractors.

The majority of workers employed by subcontractors are ''atypical'' workers — temporary, occasional — who do not enjoy the same rights as workers in a traditional employment relationship. National

---

84. In this country there has been an unprecedented increase in the number of people registered as self-employed, although there are sometimes doubts as to the exact nature of this development. Between 1981 and 1984, the number of self-employed increased by almost half a million or more than 12% of the present active population. Three-quarters of the self-employed are men working notably in distribution, the hotel trade and the construction industry.

legislatures have not yet devoted attention to them. Exceptions are a French law passed in 1977, which allows the creation of special health and safety committees which bring together representatives of the user company and the internal subcontracting companies, and an Italian law which stipulates equal pay for company workers and those employed by subcontractors.

In several member states, discussions are in progress on the possibility of devising a legal statute for subcontracting, so as to curb the abuses which it brings. In Belgium, a draft bill to this effect was filed in 1986.

MOONLIGHTING — CLANDESTINE WORK

> Man falls. Not knowing what is happening to him,
> . . . .he has just been taken away from himself.
>
> H. Michaux, *Au pays de la Magie*

Everybody knows the scale of employment in the black economy by now, but the "moonlighting" phenomenon itself evades rigorous — or even not-so-rigorous — statistical investigation. One can only guess at its extent on the basis of theories. Black-market employment eludes labour law and social security provisions, as well as the provisions of tax law. Although situated in that sector of the economy which economists call "informal" or "unstructured", black-market employment can be divided into the following categories:

— classical moonlighting, evading the legal rules and carried out mostly by native workers;

— family work, which is widespread in certain countries,[85] is carried out in the family setting, concealed by family ties, and eluding labour legislation;

— clandestine work done by foreigners, not citizens of a member state, and without residence or work permits.

Classical moonlighting seems most developed in the southern countries such as Italy or Greece, Spain and Portugal, whereas clandestine work is mostly associated with the more northerly countries: the Federal Republic of Germany, Belgium, Luxembourg.

---

85. In Greece, one-third of the active female population belongs to the category of unpaid assisting members: see Commission of the European Communities (Y. Kravaritou-Manitakis), "L'emploi des femmes en Espagne, au Portugal et en Grèce", V/2745/82 Fr, 1982.

There are also countries where the two types of employment mingle harmoniously: the United Kingdom, France. In this area of atypical employment, especially where foreign clandestine workers are involved, often the law as such is non-existent. This is an area where there is no law at all,[86/87] not merely an absence of labour and social security legislation.

The member countries — some of which already have regulations in this area (e.g. Belgium in the case of the construction industry), while others (such as the Federal Republic of Germany[88] and France[89]) have recently taken steps to combat clandestine working — should pay particular attention to the problems posed by this form of atypical employment, which is almost impossible to handle within the framework of labour and social security law. But one must be very sceptical as regards the existence of retrospective or even prospective remedies which could guarantee a minimum level of protection to clandestine workers — even though such measures would also benefit the structured sector of the economy, which suffers from the effects of this unfair competition.

---

86. One cannot avoid recalling "The Bus", a film describing the adventures of a Turkish worker taken to Sweden to work in the black economy. But there are more civilised forms of moonlighting which we have not yet noticed as regards the member countries. In one European country, which is not a member of the Community, "especially in the building trade, certain jobs are sometimes farmed out to foreign firms, even at times temporary employment agencies, who bring clandestine workers into Switzerland": Gabriel Aubert, "Les nouvelles formes et les nouveaux aspects de la relation de travail atypique", Swiss report to the Caracas conference, loc. cit., p. 140. See also R. De Grazia, *Le travail clandestin: situation dans les pays industrialisés à économie de marché*, ILO, Geneva, 1983.

87. Other questions arise here regarding human rights. One may mention Professor Evrigenis's report to the European Parliament in Autumn 1986 on "racism in the Community".

88. For Germany, see the 1981 law and *BIS* 1/1982, p. 90.

89. For France, see *BIS* 1/1983, p. 71.

III
THE EFFECTS OF THE NEW FORMS
OF WORK ON LABOUR LAW

We have already seen, and sensed, during the preceding sections, that the new forms of work have introduced unmistakable and onerous changes in the rules of labour law, and we have also seen that they are impinging on its essential functions. It should be pointed out immediately that it is not yet easy to make a precise measurement of the consequences for this branch of law caused by the developments and regulations associated with these new forms. In any case, the consequences vary, to a certain extent, from one country to another. One reason for this is undoubtedly the different "treatment" of the new forms of work by the legal system of each individual country.

In the subsections which follow, a sort of balance will be drawn up of what has already been observed in the preceding section, as regards the countries which have taken action (and those which have not taken action) on regulating atypical employment. An attempt will then be made to see what the effects are in the field of labour law, but within a rather wide perspective, without dwelling too long on the different techniques: the aim is to discover and discern the major trends. Certain effects will be pointed out on the level of individual employment relationships, such as the consequences for workers' rights regarding stability of employment, remuneration, and paid holidays. There are consequences too for the traditional employment contract, which is undergoing changes: it no longer has a monopoly of recruitment, it is becoming differentiated, it is becoming hedged in by formal requirements, and in its form as a non-permanent individual contract it poses new theoretical problems (its function, for example) which have to be resolved.

Consideration will also be given to the effects of the new forms of work on collective employment relationships.

LABOUR LAW IN MEMBER COUNTRIES FACED WITH THE NEW FORMS OF WORK

There are member countries which have taken action on the legal regulation of atypical employment. These countries are France, Italy, the Federal Republic of Germany, Spain and Belgium. The Federal

Republic of Germany through its BeschFG of 1985, France through a series of laws including the order of August 1986, and Spain through the 1984 laws, all carried out this reform by purely legislative means. In Italy and Belgium, on the other hand, there was also a certain contribution from the trade union organisations (as we shall see), or at least from the most important of them, which was important for the acceptance and legal regulation of the new forms. This was largely facilitated by collective negotiations at national level, although the nature of the negotiations was different in the two countries.

The countries which have yet to regulate the new forms of work in a more or less systematic way, either through legislation or through general negotiation, are the United Kingdom, Ireland, Denmark, the Netherlands, Greece, Luxembourg and Portugal. Here the questions raised by the new forms are settled either by means of case-law, which causes new developments in old legislation, or through company-level agreements or sometimes through agreements covering certain sectors. This is the case notably in countries belonging to the Common Law tradition: the United Kingdom and Ireland. But it is also true of Denmark, whose labour law is very close to that of the two countries just mentioned. The tradition in these countries is that legislators refrain from getting involved in the area of industrial relations. However, when one looks at the number of statutes adopted in the United Kingdom in recent years, this explanation cannot justify the inertia in this field.[1/2] In Denmark, the new forms of work have not received special attention.[3] In Portugal, the Netherlands, Greece and Luxembourg, small countries within the broad tradition of Civil Law, the legislators have not yet become involved in the area of new forms of work, except for the Portuguese law on fixed-term contracts. In the two latter countries, preparations are being made. In Luxembourg, preparatory work is well advanced; in Greece the stage of exploratory proposals has been reached. In the Netherlands, where labour law contains no major obstacles to the development of new forms of work, the proposals for reform are directed towards some very specific questions such as greater flexibility in the rules on protection for certain forms of differentiated employment.

There is a striking difference between, on the one hand, the regulation of the new forms of work by law in certain countries, where

---

1. An "inertia" which, according to some authors, is very effective and helpful to the uncontrolled expansion of these new forms, free of all regulation and any possibility of union control: see the contribution by W. Wedderburn at the Pontignano seminar. loc. cit.

2. There are suggestions by authors in this sense: see especially the article by Bob Hepple, "Restructuring Employment Rights", in *Industrial Labour Journal*, February 1986, pp. 69 ff.

3. Ruth Nielsen, "The impact ....", p. 4.

legislators have even intervened more than once, and on the other hand, at the far end of the scale (after some intermediate positions), the "ignoring" of these same forms of work, to a greater or lesser extent, by the law of the other countries among the Twelve. These differences in legal "treatment" of the new forms may be explained by various considerations: the legal system, the degree of institutionalisation of industrial relations, the power and traditions of the trade union organisations in each country, and the political set-up. Another striking factor is the hesitation and sometimes the vacillation of national legislators trying to regulate certain new forms of work — and even a tendency to step backwards both in relation to solutions worked out by case-law and in relation to previously existing legislative regulations.

HESITATIONS

It appears that it was not at all easy for legislators to recognise the typology of contracts which strip workers of traditional protection and deprive them of the "advantages" and rights which they have won. This difficulty is easily seen in the preparatory documents and even in the laws which bring new regulations to bear. Often, the following line of reasoning was followed: we don't want to, but we are forced to recognise certain new forms of work, under certain conditions, because in any case they are spreading in practice: temporary work, part-time work, fixed-term contracts. But all that we are accepting is a set of provisional regulations (France) — provisional regulations which take account of the economic crisis and of unemployment (Belgium: temporary work) — purely an experimental measure. The next stage is that the crisis continues and legislators think that it might be just as well to provide some guarantees for these new forms of work. For example: the written form of the contract, compulsory items to be specified. So the second wave of legislative intervention stabilises the effects of the first legislative action (France, Spain, Belgium, Italy), and the new forms start to look less "provisional" and exceptional. The abovementioned "difficulty" or malaise also appeared in cases where legislators were forced to do without the criteria worked out over the years by case-law, and had to impose more elastic regulations (France), or else had to suspend the application of rules established by case-law for a period of three or four years (as in the case of the Federal Republic of

Germany). In this way, almost imperceptibly, the new forms of work became part of the various legal systems, in practice on a permanent basis. And the new forms, in turn, have been causing "difficulties" in the regulations of labour law.

In any case, underneath (and despite) all the hesitations expressed on the occasions when national regulations were being adopted, one cannot but recognise that in France as in Italy, in the Federal Republic of Germany as in Spain and Belgium, there was a political will to promote the new forms of work. Whereas in some countries the "path of experimentation" is continuing — after the "provisional" introduction of temporary work in Belgium came the compromise over the trial contract (fixed-term contract), and now there are the current Hansen experiments — enough time has gone by, and our accumulated experience now makes it possible to attempt a preliminary general assessment of the effects of the new forms of work on the provisions of labour law.

A KIND OF EMPLOYMENT LAW IS BEING FORMED WHICH IMPLIES ACTION ON THE PART OF THE PUBLIC AUTHORITIES

For the countries which have taken action on regulating the new forms of work (and some fine distinctions must be drawn between the Common Law countries, and Greece and Portugal), one can see a trend towards the formation of a system of employment law which appears to give more consideration to the interests of companies than to those of the workers. This can be seen in those provisions which favour a set of differentiated employment contracts, the main feature of which is that they receive financial backing from the public authorities. This is a system of labour law which, while aiming to promote employment, only succeeds in encouraging differentiated work, while at the same time stripping it of the protection which ordinary labour law had given it. In this category of employment contracts, mainly aimed at young people and the long-term unemployed, the employer gets financial support through total or partial exemption from social security contributions: the cost of taking on these workers is partly passed on to the community.

One finds here a logic quite different from the logic of traditional labour law which, while protecting the interests of the workers and at the same time (even if this was not stated explicitly) the interests of the company, gave more consideration to protecting the workers.

In the developments just decribed one finds, firstly, that the public authorities are involved in this category of contracts under new forms, and secondly one finds that the main concern is to protect the company and encourage maximum profitability.

The "transactional" path being followed in Italy does not seem to depart from the paths followed in the other countries in order to deal with the same set of problems. In Italy, certainly, everything concerning differentiated employment contracts is more effectively monitored both by the state — the role of the labour inspectorate in drawing up certain fixed-term contracts, which does not exist anywhere else — and by the trade union organisations. And perhaps the "transaction" between the interests of workers and those of the company goes further than in other countries where the unions are weaker. In any case, it is worth noting the provision of the law which, in order to encourage part-time employment, states that the employer is no longer obliged — as had previously been the case — to employ a certain percentage of invalids. Certainly the part-time contract does have this unique quality, in relation to other new forms of contract, that it can enjoy a level of protection comparable to that of the typical contract in so far as it is not an insecure contract. It would be interesting to see whether the security which constitutes a major objective (or concern) of ordinary law and an essential characteristic of the forms could become an objective of the "transactional" path.

THE CONSEQUENCES FOR INDIVIDUAL EMPLOYMENT RELATIONSHIPS

In order to understand the context of certain consequences of the new forms of work as regards individual employment relationships, the first step will be to look at some rights of salaried employees, and the ways in which they are developing under the influence of the new forms. Next, some observations will be offered on the employment contract, which is taking on renewed interest at a theoretical level. In its new perspective, the employment contract is undergoing certain changes, and has to meet new legal concerns.

THE RIGHTS OF SALARIED WORKERS IN THE LIGHT OF NEW FORMS OF WORK

In general, since the new forms of work derogate from the protection granted by the traditional provisions of labour law, workers under new forms of contract do not enjoy the same degree of protection: they have not got equal rights with permanent employees. In several legal systems it is claimed, when atypical contracts are drawn up, that the principle of equality is being applied; but that principle has been deprived of its meaning to the extent that, for example, the level of wages paid depends on the job. If the job is part-time, or on a fixed-term, occasional, or similar basis, then there are negative implications both as regards the wages paid and as regards other rights linked to the work done and to the salary.

Protection against dismissal

The general rule is that workers under new-style contracts do not have the same protection in cases of cessation of the employment relationship, due to the completion of the term of employment, or due to the completion of the task, equivalent to that applying to typical workers as regards notice or compensation for dismissal.[4] There are differences from one country to another, and above all there are distinctions in the degree of protection between the different new forms of work.

It could be said that one group of workers under a differentiated contract have protection which remains fairly close to the traditional level; this is the group of part-time workers. In reality, however, the linkage between atypical employees and protection against dismissal reveals a more complicated picture than the simple statement that workers under new forms of contract have less protection. The search for greater flexibility in the rules governing dismissal, which can be found in all countries, expresses itself in ways which include, for example, the abolition of administrative authorisation (France), a change in the threshold of staff involving guarantees for employees against dismissal (Federal Republic of Germany), the extension of the trial period (United Kingdom: it was six months in 1979 and has now gone up to two years), and the recruitment of workers under differentiated contracts. In the Netherlands the government some years ago suggested certain "deregulations" of the protection against dismissal, which are unfavourable to atypical workers; these proposals are still under consideration. The search for flexibility is expressed even through the development of the new forms of work themselves: for example, the training contract, or early retirement. In fact, the phenomenon of differentiated employment can work on its own in

---

4. On the development of protection against dismissal in Europe, see E. Vogel, "The problem of re-employment" in B. Hepple, *The Making of Labour Law in Europe*, loc. cit., pp. 180 ff.

favour of greater flexibility in the rules on protection in cases of dismissal.

The diminution of protection seems to be carried out first of all by the recognition of the fixed-term contract: this is the case in the Federal Republic of Germany, Spain, France, Belgium, the Netherlands and also Italy. There is no doubt that certain measures, adopted in recent times, aim directly at excluding protection for certain categories of atypical employees. The German law on employment promotion, for example, rules out the existing protection in cases of dismissal for part-time workers employed for less than 45 hours per month. In Belgium too, the significant raising of the employees' salary threshold requiring advance notice and compensation for dismissal undoubtedly affects a large number of atypical workers and lowers the level of protection which they previously enjoyed.

A slightly different spirit seems, however, to pervade the new national regulations in France and Spain, which tend to grant certain "substitutes" of rights enjoyed by permanent workers to untenured workers, notably in the area of dismissals. It can be stated that whereas, in general, the protection given to workers under new-style contracts of employment varies from country to country,

— firstly, the development of new forms has had an overall effect favouring, in all countries, greater flexibility in the rules governing dismissal. In some countries, these effects have not yet been translated into the wording of statute law, but they have manifested themselves in the judgements produced by case-law;

— secondly, one can discern a trend in some countries towards the creation of "new rights" in favour of certain categories of workers on new employment contracts (i.e. untenured salaried employees), imitating those granted in cases of dismissal to workers on open-ended traditional employment contracts;

— thirdly, in this section one cannot pass over the large number of atypical workers currently on the increase — notably in Italy and the United Kingdom — represented by salaried employees who are changing over to the status of self-employed. Workers in this category have no future protection if they stop working for their employer under the guise of fake self-employed workers.

The best protected workers on an atypical contract are, as already pointed out, part-time workers employed for a duration of work which is higher than the minimum threshold prescribed in the various regulations. Under these conditions, in the United Kingdom, part-time workers have the same protection as full-time workers in cases of dismissal if they work for 16 hours per week. In Ireland, protection against dismissal requires, following the Unfair Dismissals Act of 1977, that the worker must work for at least 18 hours per week and should have worked for the same employer for at least one year. In the Netherlands all part-time workers, employed on a contract for indefinite duration, enjoy the normal protection against dismissal.

The protection of workers on a fixed-term contract of employment, at the expiry of the fixed term which automatically means the end of the employment relationship, varies from one country to another. The rule in this area is that the worker cannot be dismissed during the period of his or her contract. But after the expiry of the contract there are some countries which provide minimum protection, while others offer nothing. In the countries which have long-established regulations, such as Greece or the Federal Republic of Germany, there is no supplementary protection: neither advance warning, nor compensation for insecurity or any other reason. The legal protection offered is different in some other countries which have more modern regulations. A certain degree of protection is given after the expiry of the contract period in France, Spain, Portugal and Italy (see part two: fixed-term contract). While this regulation emancipates the fixed-term contract in relation to its former marginal position, it also emphasises the difference in protection by comparison with the traditional employment contract.

One cannot avoid emphasising, however, this new element of "gaining" some new rights on the part of workers on a fixed-term contract of employment, who in all countries have a lesser degree of protection than that given to temporary workers also on an interim contract. These rights are also granted in the assignment contracts of certain modern legislations in this area, such as the French one. The relevant provisions, however, are "double-edged": a certain amount of protection (although not enough for the insecure workers) is given by means of the "substitute" rights, but this protection consolidates the recognition of their inferior status, which is henceforth no longer considered a marginal position. It should not be forgotten, of course, that this category of non-permanent workers appear to be in a better position than the "para-subordinate" workers or those in the informal sector: the question of minimum guarantees for those working under a new form of employment which is not included within the range of employment contracts, old or new (which applies notably to the fake self-employed) still remains unresolved. These are cases where the link of subordination is not visible, or where even the job itself is concealed.

Remuneration

The lower pay levels generally received by atypical workers are another sign of the discrimination which they suffer. This question raises a multitude of problems which concern the overall system of remuneration, especially in countries where there are rules prescribing a guaranteed minimum wage. Thus in Belgium and France the employers criticise the principle of minimum wages: a differentiated system of minimum wages is sought, according to certain criteria. In the United Kingdom, the 1986 Wages Act stopped the Wages Councils from reviewing the wages of young workers aged under 21, thus effectively scrapping the minimum wage for young people. The 1987 Wages Act gives such a broad definition of remuneration, including all sorts of allowances and bonus payments, that it is certainly not going to help to improve the incomes of those who are employed under new forms of employment contract. The reality is that in the majority of member states the minimum levels, for young workers at least, have already been violated by means of various derogations: in Italy the minimum wage for young people in the craft sector is lower; in France, collective utility jobs are exempt from minimum wage levels; and so on. Young people everywhere seem to be the "chosen people" for new forms of employment.

Direct discrimination, as regards the remuneration of workers under new forms of employment, is rather rare, one of the most striking examples being the Dutch provision which deprives all workers working for less than 13 hours a week of any claim on the statutory fixed minimum wage. Discrimination is based either on practices such as subcontracting, or on the fact that even when atypical employees — on fixed-term or temporary contracts — receive the same pay, they are not allowed seniority and extra benefits due to permanent staff which are often contained in clauses of collective agreements from which temporary staff are habitually excluded. Thus, as regards workers on a fixed-term contract of employment, as the system of calculating seniority is not suited to the special circumstances of this differentiated form of employment, they seem to be receiving a "Sisyphus salary", beginning again every time on a starter rate. In the Netherlands and in the Federal Republic of Germany, part-time workers are denied compensation for overtime working. According to case-law established at the Federal Labour Tribunal, these payments must only be made if the duration of the work exceeds 40 hours. In the United Kingdom, part-time workers who get extra hours of employment have to work a higher number of hours than is required of permanent workers.

The remuneration of temporary workers in the United Kingdom, Ireland and France is not regulated. But in Belgium and Denmark it is not allowed to go below the payment received by employees with a typical employment contract and the same grade or qualification. In the Netherlands, however, the remuneration paid to this category of workers is not allowed to exceed the payment received by employees on a contract with a typical employment relationship and having the same qualification: this measure is designed to offer protection to the typical worker to avoid tensions on the labour market.

It is also known that wage discrimination against workers on a differentiated contract (as clearly shown by studies conducted by the Community into part-time working among young people) is attributable partly to their lack of qualifications and the constant interruptions in their work activities. But, as shown in the United Kingdom by the application of the 1970 Equal Pay Act (amended),[5] even when they are employed by the same employer and doing the same work, workers under differentiated contracts may face discrimination in the matter of their salaries.

In certain countries it appears that legislators have become aware of discrimination suffered by atypical employees, and are beginning to react. Thus recent legislation in Italy aimed at equal treatment compels the subcontractor to pay atypical employees the same wages as are paid to company employees.

Paid holidays, educational leave

This is an example of an attack on the rights gained by employees. The overwhelming majority of workers under new-style contracts are not in a position to fulfil the conditions which would effectively entitle them to paid holidays. Here is another instance of discrimination, given that the regulation of this right in most countries is at the service of the typical employment relationship and modelled on it.

In Ireland, under the Holiday Act of 1973, workers with a contract of employment are entitled to paid holidays provided that they have done a minimum number of hours' work. The law does not take the salary total into account. Thus, part-time workers who have worked 1400 hours during a twelve-month period (the "leave year") are entitled to a minimum of 15 days' paid holidays. If they have worked for less than twelve months, they are entitled to 1.25 days per month.

In the Netherlands, the right to paid holidays is extended to all

---

5. Paul Davies, "The Impact of New Forms of Work and Activity on Labour Law in Britain", pp. 9-10.

workers, whether typical or atypical. But the leave days granted are related to the work done. Thus part-time or fixed-term workers may not have worked for long enough to benefit from their right to paid holidays. The same is true of workers doing "odd jobs" for various employers. One exception should be mentioned: workers in the building industry can take their paid holidays independently of certain conditions which affect other workers in a negative way.

The same is true in France. The right of non-permanent workers and fixed-term or temporary employees to annual paid holidays "is reduced to a sprinkling of compensation for paid holidays"[6] handed over at the end of each contract. Paid holidays are a rarity.

In the Federal Republic of Germany, workers on fixed-term contracts lose rights which are dependent on seniority; paid holidays are part of those rights.

Discrimination is also habitually extended to the right to training and educational leave. Thus in Belgium, with the right to educational leave laid down in a law dating from 1985 — i.e. after the signature of the collective agreement on part-time working and during a period when there was a good deal of discussion on equality of rights for full-time and half-time workers — the only worker in a position to benefit from this right is one with several part-time contracts with different employers and a total duration equivalent to a full-time job. The is certainly not the case for the majority of part-time workers.

THE EFFECTS ON THE EMPLOYMENT CONTRACT

The Employment Contract no longer has a Monopoly on Recruitment

The first observation to be made on the making of employment contracts is that they no longer hold a monopoly as the means of engaging the workforce. The most important substitute technique among those which have appeared in recent years remains the company work experience programme and the training/employment contract. In several countries (Italy, Federal Republic of Germany, France, Spain) there has been new legislation on the work experience contract or apprenticeship contract and other comparable ones, facilitating and favouring controls in this area: the duration of this category of contracts has been extended, and it has been made possible

---

6. G. Lyon-Caen, "Notes sur quelques formes nouvelles", p. 17.

to repeat them several times. Given that the remuneration received by workers on a work experience, apprenticeship or training contract — according to the case and country involved — is lower than that paid to typical workers, and given that there is a reduced employer contribution to the social security system for this category of contract, employers prefer to use this type of recruitment rather than the traditional employment contract. It should be pointed out that in Spain, decree no. 1922 of 31 October 1984, which governs the training contract and the work experience contract, stipulates a reduction in employer contributions which ranges from 90% to 100% for the training contract and 75% for the work experience contract. In France, the recruitment of a young person under an adaptation contract, according to the order of 16 July 1986, gives a right to exemption from all employer contributions. But of all member countries where this kind of provision exists, Italy seems to have witnessed an unprecedented triumph for this form of atypical contract: half of all workers recruited are taken on on the basis of apprenticeship contracts.

The employment contract is becoming differentiated: not one, but several contracts

The term "employment contract" no longer conjures up the same content as it used to, because the development and recognition of new forms has meant that the employment contract is becoming differentiated: several kinds have emerged. One finds the part-time contract, the fixed-term contract, the work experience and training contract in all countries, but there also exist — as we have seen — the temporary or intermittent work contract, the alternating work contract, the job-sharing or job-splitting contract which one finds in only some of the countries in question. There are other variations also, underlining the fact that there is not one employment contract but several.

The agreement of a contract becomes surrounded by formal requirements

In all countries where legislators have regulated employment contracts under new forms, they have surrounded those contracts with formalities. They demand written records; the contract must have a written form; it must contain some compulsory stipulations. Thus the fixed-term contract in all countries — except the United Kingdom,

Ireland, Denmark, the Netherlands and Greece — is a formal contract which must specify its subject in minute detail, designate the post to be filled, contain the worker's name and qualification, and state the date of expiry when the contract is for a precise term. In cases where the cause of a fixed-term contract is a replacement or the suspension of a contract, then the fixed-term contract must also contain the name and qualification of the worker being replaced. With a fixed-term contract the duration of the contract — which varies noticeably from one country to another — must be fixed as precisely as possible. Thus in France, in cases where the parties are authorised to set an uncertain duration, they must indicate, at the time that the contract is drawn up, the event which on completion will put an end to the contractual relationship (replacement in case of illness, seasonal work), as well as a minimum duration which is freely defined.

It should also be noted that although formality is a basic feature of the fixed-term contract in all the countries mentioned — the indispensable written format, etc. — the degree of "personalisation" of the fixed-term employment contract, in relation to the compulsory specifications which it must contain, is not the same in the new-style forms of work envisaged in some recent legislation. This is the case with the fixed-term contract for "launching a new activity" described in the Spanish law no.3a of 2 August 1984 and the German law of 1985; these are fixed-term contracts designed for companies created less than six months ago and employing fewer than twenty workers.

The temporary employment contract is also surrounded — as we have seen — by formalities, especially in the Federal Republic of Germany, France and Belgium, as well as the part-time contract. The countries belonging to the Common Law tradition are an exception in this case too.

Formality: the revaluation of the individual contract

While formality shows the concern of legislators to warn the future employee that "recruitment is becoming a trap",[7] on account of the shift away from job security, it also points towards a revaluation of the individual contract. This, in its new differentiated dimension, seems in fact to be taking on a more important function than it previously had, and a more prominent position in the discipline of labour law itself.[8] It is the element of insecurity of employment

---

7. G. Lyon-Caen, "Notes sur quelques formes nouvelles", p. 17.

8. See G. Giugni's contribution in "Pontignano 3", loc. cit., p. 287.

which seems set to raise a range of new problems in the execution of employment contracts.

Execution of non-permanent contracts: dealing with suspension and seniority

The new regulations demand new responses to old techniques, such as the suspension of the contract, and seniority. There is a need to look through the laws of member states in order to see whether they already contain answers or the beginnings of answers, perhaps contained in case-law or other sources, concerning the suspension of contracts or the question of seniority in contracts under new forms distinguished by the element of insecurity.

What is the position, for example, in cases of the suspension of a temporary employment contract or fixed-term contract? Do illness or strike action constitute an extension to the termination of the assignment of a temporary worker, or an extension of the expiry date of a fixed-term contract? Can we be satisfied with the answer which is usually given, given the new extended function of non-secure contracts?

The question of seniority is even more important, as it concerns all non-permanent workers. In the new regulations (France, Spain, Italy)[9] one finds certain provisions, scattered and not systematic, which set out to ensure that an employee who gives up an insecure position and takes on a permanent job will not lose the seniority which has been built up. This problem arises particularly when a fixed-term contract is converted into an open-ended contract. As non-permanent workers in practice lose their seniority rights, this question should be totally reconsidered: "the tendency should be to calculate seniority no longer on work in a single company, but on the basis of the worker's career".[10]

At the end of a non-permanent employment contract: tendency to grant certain rights envisaged for typical workers

This tendency is found in a more marked fashion in the newest of regulations, especially those of France, Spain and Portugal, as regards fixed-term contracts. One may speak in general of a certain

---

9. More profound research should be undertaken in this area.

10. G. Lyon-Caen, op. cit.

"preoccupation" — still within the context of spreading new forms — with reproducing for non-permanent workers the situation which obtains for permanent workers. Thus we find the emergence of "compensation for end of contract" in France, in cases where a fixed-term contract draws to an end, or "compensation for insecurity of tenure" in Spain in similar circumstances (decree 1989 of 17 October 1984). In France, this same term covers compensation paid at the end of a temporary contract, which may raise certain questions connected with the determination of the employer in a triangular employment relationship, especially in cases of insolvency.

The question of accumulated contracts

Another question which needs to be dealt with in a systematic fashion is concerned with the accumulation of successive contracts of a similar or different nature (this is often the case in practice with temporary and fixed-term employment contracts). Under what conditions could such accumulation bring these workers close to the legal position of permanent staff? Italian legislation gives the following response as regards the fixed-term contract (law no.79 of 25.3.83): when a worker is recruited more than once, and the interval between the signature of the two contracts is 15 days in the case of a contract lasting under six months, and 30 days in the case of a contract lasting over six months, then the contract is transformed into an open-ended employment contract. Dutch statutory law contains a comparable provision. It is known that similar solutions are envisaged in other legal systems. This is also the position in Greek law, despite some problems of interpretation posed by recent case-law. It should be pointed out that in Belgium, although the law of 3 July 1978 sets up a legal presumption whereby parties making several successive fixed-term contracts of employment are deemed to have concluded an open-ended contract, this provision does not seem to be observed. In fact it is considered that successive contracts are permissible in cases where there is a reason justifying them.[11]

It should nevertheless be pointed out that the transformation of a fixed-term contract into an open-ended employment contract, with all the consequences that this entails for the rights of the worker involved, is implied in the logic of the penalty that the employer must suffer in cases where there is violation of legal provisions. The question in this new context, however, is not the transformation of the

---

11. See E. Vogel-Polsky, who criticises this interpretation in *Droit Social, Vol.1: Les rapports individuels du travail*, Presses Universitaires de Bruxelles, 1987, pp. 84 ff.

employment relationship, but rather the extension of certain rights designed for typical workers to workers employed under new forms of contracts.

A NEW FUNCTION OF THE CONTRACT AND THE QUESTION OF SUBORDINATION

The effects of the new forms on the employment contract are easier to understand if one also bears in mind a new function of the employment contract which is emerging most clearly in the case of employment/training contracts, but also through the extension of those types of employment contract which call into question the traditional concept of subordination. In our post-industrial era, the problem of this concept does not seem to arise exclusively in the sole case of telework.

A NEW FUNCTION OF THE EMPLOYMENT CONTRACT, THROUGH THE EMPLOYMENT/TRAINING CONTRACT

The role of the employment contract is changing, or rather growing more complex, with the new employment/training contract which has been adopted in several countries. While under the traditional contract the employee is obliged to do his or her work, bringing previously acquired occupational training to bear upon it, the employment/training contract gives the worker a chance to acquire professional training during the period of the employment contract. Young workers — the only ones affected by this type of contract in cases where they are recruited by companies which have worked out a training programme — are going to enhance their professional training or even gain additional skills. In these cases the employer has a new duty: to plan and ensure the training of the young worker.[12] One notes that the traditional objective of the employment contract — the performance of the contracted work — may now be accompanied by other objectives, such as the completion or acquisition of occupational training. This new function of the employment contract is attributable to government policy on promoting youth employment while assisting companies. The state's aspirations in the area of job promotion are also expressed in part-time and fixed-term employment contracts for workers previously registered as

---

12. See the report by Bruno Venezani at the Jesolo conference (September 1986) on ''New technology and the contract of employment''.

unemployed, now sharing their jobs with people on early retirement schemes. One also notes, in connection with this type of development in labour law, that it is aiming more to promote employment than to ensure its continuity, which was previously its main objective.

THE EMPLOYMENT CONTRACT WHICH CALLS INTO QUESTION THE TRADITIONAL CONCEPT OF SUBORDINATION

While mention has been made of the formality now surrounding the employment contract, as one effect of the new forms of work, it should also be added that, in rather the opposite sense, another effect is the extension of employment contracts which call into question the traditional concept of subordination. This is true notably of contracts for home-based work and telework. The extension of these forms goes hand in hand with the trend towards externalisation of labour.

It is true that in several member states[13] one can see a trend, not yet clearly expressed, towards moving beyond the traditional concept of subordination, which no longer seems appropriate to cover certain categories of workers who do their jobs at a distance: outside the company, but on behalf of the company. The traditional concept of subordination really seems to be tending not to disappear but rather to be replaced, after a sort of explosion, by a series of different kinds of subordination which go with different types of work. It is also being replaced by different kinds of subordination, if one considers the phrase coined by the two Italian authors[14] who wrote of home-based working, or rather of the homeworker: "This is the most subordinated of para-subordinate workers, and at the same time the least subordinated of subordinate workers." But it is true that the Italians have developed this concept of "parasubordinazione",[15] which does not exist in other countries although one can find the same problems which gave rise to it. The theoretical and practical importance of redefining and re-shaping the traditional concept of subordination can only be understood if one takes account of the dimensions of the current movement towards a "self-employed status" for employees, as already mentioned, which is a reversal of the earlier trend in Europe

---

13. See the contributions in "Pontignano III", loc. cit., p. 285. The United Kingdom is included in its statement, despite the special features of its labour law. See also Bob Hepple, "Restructuring Employment Rights", *Industrial Labour Journal*, 1986, pp. 67 ff.; see p. 71 for the case of "the three 'regular casual' waiters".

14. G. Ghezzi, U. Romagnoli, *Il rapporto di lavoro*, 2nd edition, Zanichelli, Bologna, p. 32.

15. Op. cit., pp. 28-29; but see also Maria-Vittoria Ballestrero, "L'ambigua nozione di lavoro parasubordinato", *Lavoro e Diritto*, January 1987, pp. 41 ff.

— the traditional movement of the 19th and 20th centuries — whereby certain economically weak and dependent self-employed workers were treated as subordinate workers and taken into the ranks of wage-earners. The new trend consists rather in the fact that a large number of workers, although subordinate and salaried, find themselves externalised in relation to the company and are frequently considered as self-employed although this is not the case.

Finally, while in almost all countries unity of place and work is no longer indispensable in classifying a job as subordinate and applying protective legislation, it is necessary to look every time for criteria that allow this classification. It is no mere chance if — as we have seen under the appropriate heading where the legal rules for home-based working are discussed (chapter II, 2.6.) — the legal status of this work is fluid and ambiguous. In this context, particular interest attaches to the proposals which, in classifying employment contracts, consider the element of "organisation" which makes it possible to identify the connection between the worker and the company, the type of employment, and the legal protection which is applicable.

EFFECTS ON COLLECTIVE WORK RELATIONSHIPS

COLLECTIVE RIGHTS UNDER THE NEW FORMS OF EMPLOYMENT

Labour law in the member states, centred on the traditional employment contract — open-ended duration, full-time, etc. — mostly concerned with industrial workers and "surprised" by the pace of recent developments, has not yet been able to develop and integrate, systematically across the full range of member states, the (non-existent) union activities of those workers whose links with their companies are weak. This means that workers on a non-permanent contract, home-based workers and teleworkers, the fake self-employed and the "parasubordinated" workers, despite the fact that their employment relationship is provided for and regulated by law, do not in principle enjoy the collective rights of workers having a typical employment relationship.

The weakening of the trade union organisations during these recent years which have been so encouraging to the development of new forms of work, is certainly one of the reasons for the weakening of the exercise of collective rights. The general atmosphere, among other things, was not favourable to the extension of collective rights to atypical employees. It must also be added that workers under new forms of work, as a rule, do not have the same "consciousness" as the traditional worker. They are characterised by a very different mentality from that of typical workers.[16] The lack of a global strategy among the trade unions in relation to atypical employment — given the time that it took them to accept that this phenomenon was a permanent development — is another reason. But this does not seem to be the case any more.[17] In addition, there is a growing awareness in many countries of the need for an effective extension of collective rights to atypical workers. Already, for example, the labour law of certain member states is providing for the extension of some collective rights.

The collective relationships of workers under the new forms of work bring together several types of interest, both for permanent employees and for workers under new forms of employment. Here it should simply be pointed out, before proceeding to a very brief description of some national regulations, that legislation in certain countries (the Federal Republic of Germany, Belgium, Holland) obliges an employer to inform the works council of his or her intention to recruit a number of non-permanent workers.

NATIONAL REGULATIONS

There are countries which take no account of the collective rights of workers with an atypical employment relationship — in particular, their participation in representative bodies. This is especially true of countries which have not produced an overall systematic set of regulations for new forms of work and activity: Greece, Ireland, the United Kingdom and Portugal. But it is not true of countries such as France, Italy or Spain, which have given certain forms of atypical employment their own special legal regulations.

Thus the Spanish law of 1984, while recognising the principle of equal and proportional treatment for part-time workers, makes explicit reference to the enjoyment of union rights by this category of atypical employees too. The same is true of other categories of atypical workers under contract. The rule in Spain is that these people should have the same collective rights as workers in a typical employment relationship. In calculating the staff numbers of a company, workers with a fixed-term contract exceeding twelve months in duration are

---

16. See Efren Cordova, Summary report on the theme of "atypical employment", loc. cit.

17. See Mathias Hinterscheid, "Le rôle du travail, des travailleurs et de leurs syndicats dans la société de demain", loc. cit., p. 11.

taken into account. So as to be able to count part-time workers among the company staff, the following yardstick is used: a global calculation is made, including part-time employment contracts, and every time that a sum of 200 working days is reached, it is deemed that another extra staff member may be added to the permanent staff count of the company.

In the Netherlands, recent amendments on the legislation on works councils, which dates from 1950, have opened the possibilities of atypical workers participating in this system. Joint committees in each sector of industry can further increase this involvement, but this power is rarely used. However, there remain many impediments preventing atypical workers from participating in the Dutch system of works councils, such as the requirement of a certain period of service.[18]

On the other hand, in Belgium the legislation on works councils and health and safety committees does not make the timetable of work done a criterion for conferring voting rights or eligibility. In this area no distinction is drawn between workers employed full-time and those working part-time.

In Ireland there is no legislation on a works council or committee. Worker representation is carried out by trade union organisations. Although they are eligible, atypical employees seldom figure among those elected to company union positions. Representatives must be employees on a full-time basis. This is, incidentally, one of the conditions required by a 1977 law on worker participation in public utility companies (the Worker Participation Act). The presence of atypical employees in trade union bodies in sectors employing a high proportion of them (e.g. part-time commercial workers) is desirable. Equally desirable is that part-time workers should be counted among company staffs in connection with all forms of participation. In this country, at any rate, the development of new forms of work has not apparently had as negative an impact on the activities and organisations of the trade union movement as in the United Kingdom.

In the United Kingdom, where the government's encouragement of new forms of work as part of its policy of weakening the trade unions has without a shadow of a doubt done union activity no good at all, the collective rights of workers do not appear to enjoy any special importance. This is partly due to the fact that British law has not worked out any system of representation for workers through workers' councils or committees. Thus, one can hardly raise the problem of worker participation in non-existent bodies. But the

---

18. Christe Dienand, "New forms and aspects of atypical employment relationships", Dutch report to the Caracas conference, loc. cit., p. 37.

question of collective rights does arise all the same, in cases where certain rules of individual employment law apply to employees only. The rules involved may indeed concern union representatives: where it is illegal for an employer to dismiss or victimise a worker for belonging to a trade union, these rights are confined to employees alone.[19] Should they not also be extended to atypical workers? Of course this question may seem naive in the context of British law. The situation is different as regards the Federal Republic of Germany.

Before the reform, German law stated that worker representation was prescribed in all establishments employing more than five workers, without distinguishing between those on a part-time contract and others. The new legislation, however, stipulates that the company staff must be taken as including those part-time workers who are employed for at least 10 hours per week and 45 hours per month. This new legislation has nothing to say on the exercise of the collective rights of atypical employees as regards, for example, their participation in the works council. It thus seems desirable that the legislators, if they take on the task of regulating atypical employment, should also deal with these questions instead of referring them back to the general legal system.

The special features of the exercise of collective rights by atypical workers, although they are not the same for all categories of atypical workers, deserve the attention of legislators in the Federal Republic of Germany, and of trade union organisations too in countries where collective agreements are the prime source of labour law.

In France, following recent legislation, the various forms of non-permanent employment are counted in calculating staff numbers:

(a) Employees under a fixed-term contract, employees under an intermittent contract, and workers supplied including temporary workers are counted in the staffing totals of the company, proportionate to the amount of time that they have been present in the company during the preceding twelve months.

(b) Part-time employees count in calculating staff through the division of the sum total of timetables appearing in the employment contract by the duration of work as established by law or by agreement. Before 1986 they used to be counted in their entirety.

(c) In France, home-based workers are counted in their entirety among company staff.

---

19. The same is true of the employer's right to consult a recognised trade union organisation on a proposed dismissal or company transfer: these measures apply to employees only, not to people engaged under a "contract for services". On the other hand, the law on industrial disputes covers all "workers", whether or not they are "employees".

Despite the differences between recent national regulations, there is quite a clear trend towards recognising the right of atypical employees to be considered among staff totals, to participate in general assemblies, and to stand for election to representative bodies. But the traditional logic of extending the rights of typical employees to atypical employees is not suitable for all groups of atypical workers. How can fake self-employed workers (parasubordinate workers) or teleworkers express their collective rights? Certainly, priority should not be given to inventing new regulations, but to atypical workers themselves developing an awareness of their collective rights. Their very poor rate of unionisation, and the absence of union activity of their own, could be seen as arguments in favour of measures of this type. The following section will present, in spite of all this, a view of the exercise of collective rights by teleworkers.

COLLECTIVE RIGHTS AND TELEWORKERS: PERSPECTIVES

There is a need to redefine the conditions for the exercise of collective rights for each new category of workers arriving on the employment scene. One should also be able to take advantage of new conditions and special features in the telework sector.

If teleworkers work under the same position of subordination as the other workers in a company, and are treated in the same way, then:

(a) they must be taken into consideration in calculating the indispensable number of workers required for setting up representative bodies — the works council or committee, the safety and health committee or union council, depending on the country involved;

(b) they have the right to be candidates for election to the works council;

(c) they obviously have the right to vote in such elections.

Under these conditions, teleworkers can move away from the isolation which is partially inherent in the nature of their work, and participate actively in the life of the company, advancing their shared aspirations. But teleworkers can use other means of contact and communication between themselves. The very nature of their work could make it possible, for example, to distribute a company electronic newspaper which would keep them informed on company and union affairs. The use of new technology could certainly operate to enhance collective rights and their exercise, at least in the case of workers in the telework sector. Labour law should be equipped with appropriate provisions to encourage, among other things, the circulation of information by accessing telework links, and also to allow workers' representatives to have access to the electronic resources of telework, connected to company databanks. One could also envisage the possibility of information exchange among work representatives by means of their video display terminals.[20] There are further possibilities for exercising collective rights which could be envisaged through the use of teleworkers' screens. Telework launches a challenge to collective labour rights, but the situation must also be grasped by the union organisations and the workers.

20. R. Lemesle, "Le télétravail: contribution à l'élaboration de dispositions internes et de normes internationales spécifiques de droit du travail", op. cit. One can easily imagine such co-ordination between representatives of the workers in a European multinational such as Philips, or a multinational with a number of establishments in the member countries.

IV
THE EFFECTS OF THE NEW FORMS
OF WORK ON SOCIAL SECURITY LAW

> "One sees the cage, one hears the fluttering,
> one registers the unmistakable noise of the beak
> being sharpened against the bars. But no birds."
>
> H. Michaux, *Au pays de la Magie*

THE NEW FORMS IN SOCIAL SECURITY LAW: BADLY INTEGRATED

It is a commonplace observation that social security law in the member states, independently of the different systems of financing which they use — contributions or taxes — is failing to keep pace with developments brought about by the new forms of work.[1] These are undoubtedly incorporated in the social system, notably when they arise through one of the contracts of the previously mentioned new typology. In the majority of member countries social security liability goes well beyond the employment contract: whatever the form or title of the contract, once there is an employment relationship, social security liability comes into play. The social security system, however, is used to dealing mostly with traditional social risks — illnesses, old-age pensions, etc. — and has not yet taken a systematic and comprehensive approach to the new social risks engendered by the new forms, which have arisen in about the last fifteen years and have shown constant growth. Certainly, an attempt has been made during that time to look at the special needs for social protection among certain groups of atypical workers. This was done notably by taking a serious interest in one of the atypical forms of employment, part-time working. Thus it became clear that this branch of law has remained anchored to outmoded preconceptions, such as the notion that unemployment is a non-permanent state, or outmoded concepts

---

1. See Commission of the European Communities, "Problèmes de Sécurité Sociale: thèmes d'intérêts communs", (communication to the Council) COM 86, 410 final. See Brussels meeting reports, pp. 27 ff.; Xavier Prelot, "La Sécurité Sociale en Europe", *Droit Social*, January 1987, pp. 70 ff.

which do not apply in other sectors, such as for example the concept of the head of the family.

An awareness of these problems in connection with part-time working led in certain countries, as in the characteristic case of the United Kingdom, to a new policy and reforms in the matter of half-time working, an atypical form which is very strongly feminised and also linked to the area of family training. Now, in most member states,[2] the new regulations and measures concerned with part-time working and temporary and non-tenured employment generally, being fragmentary and designed for particular situations, usually reflect nothing more than the desire of member states to provide exemptions in the field of social security in order to strengthen the competitiveness of their economies in a period of crisis. The atypical workers are subjected to the effects of this government policy, and also (as we have seen) to the effects of the new company policy of replacing workers on traditional contracts, who are guaranteed maximum protection by the social security system, with workers on an atypical employment contract. Independently of the solutions provided by government policies and company policies, which are undoubtedly short-term policies and measures, the social security and protection systems of member states — and, at Community level, in the context of the trend towards harmonising social security systems — should approach the new forms of work as a new phenomenon which is destined to expand. It is a phenomenon of the future because it can also express a personal choice by workers: the option of reducing

---

2. In order to give an idea of the rates of expenditure for social protection in each country — a question which was raised at the group meeting in Brussels — the following table is reproduced here.

Table 1:   **Social protection expenditure as a percentage of GNP in member states for the year 1983**

Country	Percentage
Federal Republic of Germany	30.2
Belgium	31.9
Denmark	28.9
Greece*	20.2
Spain*	18.5
France	28.8
Ireland	24.6
Italy	27.3
Luxembourg	29.3
Netherlands	34.0
Portugal*	12.6
United Kingdom	23.7

*The table is based on OECD data for all countries except Greece, Spain and Portugal, where the data are from national sources. See Commission of the European Communities, COM (86) 410 final, Annex 2.

the place of work in one's life, so as to give a more prominent place to other activities and aspirations: to live one's personal and family life better, to express oneself creatively outside the work situation, to carry on an unpaid social or other activity at the same time: in short, to enhance one's living conditions. For the moment, however, atypical employment is not a free choice for the great majority of workers in this category: the choice is conditioned by a minimum level of protection which ensures ''survival'' — the reproduction of workers themselves — according to needs historically determined by the Western European society in which they live. Atypical employment is still imposed in a coercive way on workers in this category.

In an entirely preliminary approach to the consequences of the development of new forms of work on social security law — an inadequate approach, for a variety of reasons[3] — we present some responses given by the social security systems of member states to atypical employment, which will allow us to appreciate the context of certain problems posed by ''new social risks'' and to identify some trends. An attempt will be made to identify the position of atypical workers in the system of social protection: are they closer to workers with a typical contract, or to the ''new poor'' who are also appearing in the Community? In this sense, are they marginal — with a sizeable involvement in the social assistance services — or do they to a large extent form a special category which imposes a revision of not only the arrangements but also certain principles of the social security system? These might include, for example, the conditions on which rights are forfeited, the differences in the treatment of the long-term unemployed, the role of occupational training, the non-penalisation of the unemployed.

UNEMPLOYMENT INSURANCE: CALCULATED ON THE BASIS OF FORMER EARNINGS, IT IS NOT SUITED TO ATYPICAL EMPLOYMENT

The most significant risk facing atypical workers is unemployment, given that the major problem is under-employment, chronic unemployment (non-secure or part-time). Although the conditions

3. N.B. The contributions for the preparation of this report were provided by labour law specialists. Now, as Mr Calderbank of the Commission of the European Communities emphasised at the meeting of 17 October (see report, pp. 98-99), experts in social security law are already taking an interest in certain forms of atypical employment, notably part-time working, and social security law. Although they have not yet studied the phenomenon of atypical work in general, they are far better qualified to undertake the study of the effects of the new forms of work on social security law. Thus, this part of the report is being written within the limitations imposed by these conditions.

which a worker must fulfil in order to benefit from an unemployment allowance are not the same in all member states, one can see some points in common.[4] Firstly, as the periods during which workers are entitled to receive unemployment benefit are limited, these rights are quickly exhausted. Secondly, as benefits are calculated on the basis of previous earnings and on a certain reference period, they are always lower than those received by typical workers. As will be seen through the examples cited, unemployment benefits are really designed for traditional typical workers.

In Denmark, the unemployment insurance system is a voluntary one, managed by the insurance funds. Workers who work for between 15 and 30 hours per week may be admitted as part-time insured persons. The maximum amount of allowances which they can receive is equivalent to two-thirds of the allowances which are payable to full-time insured workers.

In Ireland, social security contributions are directly related to earnings, while short-term benefits are paid at a standard rate. In this context, unemployed part-time workers and non-permanent workers receive lower rates of unemployment benefit by comparison with workers in a typical employment relationship. It should be pointed out that the Irish social security system will not cover an insubstantial job (less than 18 hours' work, or with earnings under a certain level) except in cases where the livelihood of workers depends on their earnings from an insubstantial job.

In the unemployment insurance system of the Federal Republic of Germany, a lower threshold is set for part-time workers. German

---

4. The limited proportion represented by unemployment benefits in relation to the total of social security benefits, but also in relation to those covering other risks (for example, old age), may be clearly seen from the table below.

Table 2 **Percentage of total social security benefits for health, old age, family, unemployment and other functions**

Country	Health	Age	Family	Unemp.	Other	Total
FRG	27.0	29.8	6.5	7.1	29.6	100
Belgium	21.9	27.0	9.9	14.2	27.0	100
Denmark	23.5	34.3	9.4	13.7	19.1	100
Spain*	29.0	42.0	0.02	15.0	9.0	100
Greece*	18.7	70.3	3.3	2.7	5.5	100
France	24.7	34.0	9.6	9.8	21.9	100
Ireland	29.0	24.9	9.4	13.1	23.6	100
Italy	22.5	34.7	6.9	3.2	32.7	100
Luxembourg	22.5	26.7	7.6	8.1	10.6	100
Netherlands	25.8	27.0	8.1	12.7	26.6	100
UK	20.3	40.6	10.6	10.1	18.4	100

*The table is based on OECD data for all countries except Greece, Spain and Portugal, where the data are from national sources. See Commission of the European Communities, COM (86) 410 final, Annex 2.

social security law makes the receipt of benefits offered for unemployment or other risks conditional on taking a continual paid occupational training course.[5] It is generally accepted by the legal system in this country that temporary cessation of work does not imply an automatic suspension of the employment relationship, if the worker continues to receive his or her salary. The question arises, on the other hand, as to whether the employment relationship remains a remunerated relationship in cases where a worker's part-time job involves the temporary abolition by the worker of his or her obligation to work, together with the accompanying right to a salary. An interruption in the salary extending beyond four consecutive weeks has a damaging effect on the right to benefits from unemployment insurance.

It should be pointed out, moreover, that continual attendance at a paid employment course does not involve automatic liability of the worker to compulsory insurance, if certain minimum conditions are not met: according to paragraph 102 of the employment promotion law ("Arbeitsförderungsgesetz"), the worker must be employed for at least 19 hours in order to receive unemployment benefits.

In Luxembourg, the law of 30 June 1976 stipulates (article 11, subsection 2) that the insurance of workers employed on a part-time basis is conditional on each unemployed worker having done at least 20 hours' work. Workers who work less than 20 hours receive no compensation because — as the parliamentary debates show — there was a concern to prevent the creation of a category of "artificial unemployed".

In the United Kingdom, part-time workers and non-permanent workers are entitled to unemployment benefit on the following conditions: their remuneration must have reached a certain level (£35 sterling), and they must have paid contributions for at least 50 weeks of the financial year. In this case they are entitled to unemployment benefit for a period of twelve months. It should be pointed out that a recipient of unemployment benefit is entitled to carry on a limited job which does not amount to a "principal activity". Workers whose earnings fall below the minimum required are free to pay voluntary contributions, but these do not entitle them to unemployment benefit (they will be entitled to a retirement pension and certain other benefits which do not include either health or maternity benefit, nor invalidity benefit). There is one category of atypical workers, the part-time employees (the great majority of whom are women), who up to 1978 did not pay contributions at the full rate and were thus deprived of

---

5. Falkenberg, op. cit.

their rights. Since then, with the new legislation (EPCA) and new policies in this area, the number of part-time and non-permanent workers entitled to unemployment benefit has increased by 150%. But at the same time, there is a number of part-time and non-permanent workers falling short of minimum income during the reference year, although while working they are above the threshold; they are excluded from the social security system and deprived of the benefits to which they could become entitled. These workers may receive "supplementary benefits", a form of assistance which is not the same as "contributory benefits", but this lies outside the scope of social security law in the strict sense.

In France, unemployment benefit is calculated on the basis of previous earnings. When a worker employed on a part-time contract works for a very small number of hours, he or she receives a reduced unemployment benefit. Non-permanent employees, who have worked under a fixed-term contract, or as temporary or intermittent staff, are supposed to receive unemployment benefit, but a period of three months' membership of the scheme during the preceding year — in one or more companies — may present an obstacle here. Being unemployed does not give one the right to expect unemployment benefit. Moreover, there is a period of delay which can militate against workers between two assignments, or against intermittent workers. Even in cases where non-permanent workers satisfy all the conditions which entitle them to receive unemployment benefit, the benefit itself will quite possibly be a small one. It is all very well for French law to assert, each time that it takes an interest in atypical forms of employment, that there are equal rights for all employees;[6] but this has not prevented the unemployment insurance system, in France as elsewhere, from being designed for people in permanent jobs, or for the category of long-term unemployed.[7]

The recently-revised Dutch Unemployment Benefit Scheme, however, is no longer specifically designed for people in permanent jobs. All workers are entitled to the benefit as soon as they suffer a substantial loss of wages. However, benefits are still calculated on the basis of previous earnings, so the benefit of many atypical workers would be small. Moreover, benefits will often only be granted if a certain period of insurance has been fulfilled, a certain minimum number of days has been worked or a certain minimum wage has

---

6. See J. Pelissier, "La relation de travail atypique", *Droit Social* no.7, July/August 1985, pp. 531 ff.

7. G. Lyon-Caen, "Notes sur quelques nouvelles formes d'emploi", p. 20.

been earned — three requirements which clearly disadvantage many atypical workers.

Unemployment insurance, taking as its model the requirements of typical workers, is pervaded by a rigidity which is not well suited to the types of social risks which face workers under new forms of contract. The system has not adapted to the requirements of differentiated employment.

OTHER SOCIAL BENEFITS

In all member states, non-permanent workers and part-time workers receive salaries which are lower than those paid to typical employees; and non-permanent workers also have difficulties in fulfilling the condition of previous duration of affiliation. As social security benefits are always a function of earnings, apart from some rare exceptions, atypical workers:

— always receive lower and often minimal benefits, i.e. insufficient to cover the risk which is faced;

— are excluded from a number of social security benefits in certain countries.

Thus, in the United Kingdom, for a worker to receive the complete range of benefits conferred by the social security system, he or she must pay contributions which amount to about "one fifth of the average salary of a male manual worker", for a duration of 50 weeks per fiscal year. If atypical workers are not in a position to contribute during this period, they may receive benefits at a reduced rate if they cover half of it, or 25 weeks. There is also provision for another, third-class category: when the remuneration of atypical employees is so low that they cannot pay the minimum contribution required, then they are entitled to pay a voluntary contribution which gives them the right to a retirement pension and certain other benefits, but not to illness benefit, nor maternity benefit, nor yet unemployment or invalidity benefit. As we know, however, there are also supplementary allowances in the United Kingdom, based on the well-organised system of social assistance. The rights of atypical employees may be even more limited in countries which apply the remuneration principle fairly severely, as is done in the Federal Republic of Germany.

It is worth mentioning a change in the law in Italy, which certainly does nothing for workers employed under new forms of contract (the particular category involved being part-time workers). Under the previously existing system, a minimum level of social charges was expected from the employer, independently of the number of hours actually worked by the employee. The content of this principle was justified by the need to provide social security funds with the necessary financial resources to allow them to fulfil their functions.

After the reform, the minimum level of social charges paid by the employer is reduced by comparison with the charges payable for a typical worker. Part-time workers with a daily timetable of less than 4 hours are left outside the system. Thus, the principle applying to full-time workers, according to which lower earnings are matched by higher social charges, has been replaced by the principle that lower earnings correspond to lower social charges. This principle favours neither the workers nor the social institutions, but merely the companies. This does not seem like a path to follow in order to resolve the new set of problems, as it leads to a "one-dimensional" law which offers protection only to the company.

In the context of the development of these questions, one is aware of the fertile ground which is being prepared for private insurance companies, which can flourish at the expense of the national social security systems. One may mention here the Irish case: in Ireland, only workers employed under a service contract, and insured according to the Social Welfare (Consolidation) Act, 1981, are entitled to the full range of social benefits. The full list of benefits includes invalidity benefit, illness benefit, maternity benefit, death benefit, and others. In principle, all workers with an employment contract are supposed to be covered by social security, regardless of the size of their earnings. In fact, however, part-time workers and temporary employees who work for less than 18 hours per week find themselves covered in a different category, known as Class J.[8] This is a type of second-class insurance, which provides only for the risks of unemployment and illness.

ILLNESS AND MATERNITY

It is unusual for atypical employees to be entitled to compensation for illness and maternity. Where such entitlement exists, the allowances paid, which are calculated on the basis of remuneration

---

8. Part-time workers can belong to the first category of insured persons (Class A) if they can prove that their job is not of a subsidiary nature and inconsiderable extent.

received, are firstly and in all cases lower than those paid to workers with a typical employment relationship. They are reduced even in countries such as Denmark where everybody is entitled to illness and maternity benefits, because they are not linked to a professional activity. In the other countries — the majority — benefits of this type may be very low indeed, in other words insufficient to cover the risks effectively. In certain countries such as Greece, maternity is no longer classified as an illness — in fact, when one thinks of it, human reproduction is devalued when social security law treats childbirth like a disease — and the qualifications for obtaining maternity allowances are more favourable (100 days rather than 200) so that an entitlement to a maternity allowance can be established. However, it is still necessary for atypical workers to be able to fulfil these more favourable conditions. Apart from women who work part-time on very short timetables, or temporary or occasional women workers, those who carry on an independent profession or work in an auxiliary capacity are also deprived of holidays and maternity allowances. The emergence of the trend, observed in several countries, towards the separation of rights from the typical or atypical nature of the employment relationship, could be seen as expressing an egalitarian social security policy.

In the United Kingdom, atypical employees who do not reach the required threshold are excluded from statutory sick pay. And as the British labour market is more and more populated by atypical workers on a permanent basis, these workers are increasingly tending to be insured by their employers through private insurance companies. In Britain too, atypical employees who do not reach the ''threshold'' when working on a part-time basis, holding a non-permanent job, or carrying on a self-employed business, are not entitled to maternity leave and maternity allowances.

In Denmark, on the other hand, the entire population receives benefits in kind in cases of illness or maternity. In spite of everything, these benefits in kind are linked to workers' earnings. Benefits in kind can reach as high as 90% of income and are withheld only in cases where they represent 10% of the maximum value of benefits. These provisions cover the majority of part-time workers and those with non-permanent jobs, because even with 4 hours' work per week the employee is entitled to certain benefits, however modest these may be.

In Luxembourg, the health insurance system does not allow affiliation to be denied on the basis of the limited number of working hours, except in the case of an occasional job where the worker, employed in domestic service, is working for fewer than 16 hours. However, the amount of benefit is very low for workers who have worked on a part-time basis with a limited timetable, and very low too for non-permanent workers.

In France, all workers are entitled to illness and maternity insurance. In calculating the benefits, which are certainly lower than those received by traditional workers and can at times be very low indeed, reference is made to the entire salary received by the insured person. The condition for establishing rights remains that which applies to all full-time employees on open-ended contracts: showing the completion of the requisite 200 hours' work per three-month period. Atypical workers who do not satisfy this required duration have the option of insuring themselves voluntarily with private insurance firms.

In the Netherlands all workers receive benefits in cases of illness or maternity, but these are related to the previous earnings and can therefore be small for numerous atypical workers. Affiliation to this scheme, however, is denied to some atypical workers, those working less than two days a week or earning less than 40% of the minimum wage. After one year of illness two other social security schemes become effective instead. The first scheme covers the entire population, and guarantees a basic benefit without differentiating as to the character of the job. The second scheme provides for additional benefits, but only to workers, and related to previous earnings.

In Ireland, maternity leave — which was previously almost unknown — was established by the 1981 Maternity Protection Employment Act. This law, setting up a right to unpaid maternity leave, and for medical care before and after the birth, is applied, however, only to workers on a permanent contract of employment or contract of service, who work for at least 18 hours per week, or else workers on a fixed-term contract lasting for at least 26 weeks.[9/10] Thus, part-time and non-permanent employees working less than 18 hours per week are not entitled to maternity leave; the same is true of casual employees.

In the Federal Republic of Germany, under paragraph 311, subsection 1, no.1 of the state social insurance order (Reichsversicherungsordnung RVO), the worker does not sacrifice his or her membership of the health insurance scheme even if he or she is in a non-remunerated employment relationship for three consecutive weeks. The right to benefit is however lost if the worker's employment contract provides for an interruption of remuneration for a period exceeding three weeks. Arising frequently in cases of

---

9. This law also guarantees the right to return to work after maternity leave. See K. Asmal, "The impact", op. cit., p. 18.

10. It is sometimes a practice among employers who use a large number of part-time workers, independently of the hours worked.

flexible work, the loss of benefit is not without legal remedy. The temporary exclusion of the part-time worker from protection offered by illness insurance may be avoided if the worker is paid a salary averaged over the month, with the level determined by the reduced duration of the work done.[11] Apart from the case already mentioned, German law also excludes workers whose salary level and work duration fall below a certain threshold from receiving benefits provided by illness and old age insurance. In particular, this includes employees working for less than 15 hours per week with a salary not exceeding 400 DM.

OCCUPATIONAL ACCIDENTS

There are countries which adapt the temporary work incapacity compensation system to the requirements of part-time working. Thus, if at the moment of the accident the victim is carrying on a part-time job, the base salary for calculating the temporary work incapacity compensation is set in relation to the wages due for the part-time job. It is, however, difficult to accept this logic in cases where the worker, following the accident, is struck by permanent total disability: the disability is not partial merely because the worker held a part-time job.[12] Compensation calculated proportionately to a half or quarter salary would not be sufficient to cover the consequences of this risk. This reasoning means that in Italy — which seems to offer an example of the most promising development — when calculating the amount of contributions due from atypical employees on part-time contracts, the basis taken is not the amount of salary actually received, but rather the corresponding full-time salary. This allows part-time workers to have the same protection as typical workers in case of accident (or occupational illness).

The case of an occupational accident affecting a temporary worker may also serve as a classic case demonstrating the unsuitability of the system for covering social risks in dealing with atypical forms of work. This is true in France and elsewhere: occupational risks exist in the user company, but the temporary employment agency is the worker's only employer.

---

11. Däubler, *Das Arbeitrecht*, 2, p. 803.

12. See the contribution by E. Vogel to the Brussels meeting, and her proposals in favour of calculating benefits on the basis of a fictional salary, which would conform to the principle of equal treatment, pp. 118-121. In the Netherlands, this unsatisfactory result is partly corrected by a social security scheme, covering the whole population, which after one year of illness provides a basic benefit irrespective of the previous earnings.

FAMILY ALLOWANCES

In several member countries, the rights to family allowances[13] are conditional on occupational activity, and the amount paid also depends on the rate of contributions. In these countries — the Federal Republic of Germany, Belgium, Italy, Greece, Spain and Portugal — atypical workers are disadvantaged. Either they are entitled to family allowances on a lower level than that payable to workers on a typical contract, or else they do not receive such allowances at all. In certain member states, the law in this area is adapted to the atypical forms of employment. This is the case in Belgium. The changes made in 1981 stipulate that family allowances are payable for each working day effectively made up of at least three hours (previously the minimum was four hours). When the number of days effectively worked during a month rises to at least 16 (or 80 hours), a flat-rate allowance is payable. Unemployed persons voluntarily accepting a short-time job are also entitled to family allowances. In Italy, part-time workers receive family allowances for the full week, provided that they have worked for at least 24 hours.

In several member states, however, there is a tendency to dissociate the payment of family allowances from occupational activity. The demographic position in Europe would favour this policy on family allowances.[14] In certain countries such as France, the Netherlands and Denmark, indeed, this dissociation is already a fact.[15] In Denmark, the right to family allowances is not conditional on occupational activity (but on residence), and the allowances are fully financed out of public funds. In France too, the right to family allowances is not subject to any conditions about work activity. The same is true of Luxembourg, where the entitlement to family allowances derives not from the job but from the child. Family allowances dissociated from occupational activity would also be favourable to atypical workers.

---

13. As shown by Table 2, the proportion of benefits paid to the family out of the total social protection benefits varies from one country to another: 10.6% in the United Kingdom, 0.02% in Spain. The two most important demographic phenomena, which are the drop in the birthrate to a historically unprecedented level (1982: 2.1 children in all member countries with the exception of Ireland: 2.95), and the rise in the number of single-parent families in all countries, with the head of household usually being the mother, demand a new — and generous — policy on family benefits.

14. See the report to the Economic and Social Committee on the demographic situation in member states, Brussels, June 1985.

15. This is another question: the relative decline in family allowances which comes up against the policy demanded by the worrying problem of an ageing population.

PENSIONS: PENSIONS FOR WORKERS UNDER NEW FORMS OF EMPLOYMENT CONTRACT ARE NOT GUARANTEED — APART FROM THE SOCIAL SECURITY PENSION

In the majority of member countries, retirement pensions are dependent on a minimum of existing affiliation and contributions.

The facts that most atypical workers do not work full-time during the reference period, and that they have periods of inactivity — apart from the low pay which they generally receive — have repercussions on the amount of their pensions. The pension rate in countries which apply a strict remunerative principle, as in the case of the Federal Republic of Germany, can be very small and thus insufficient to meet the worker's needs. Indeed it can even be non-existent. This is not the case, however, in countries providing a social pension, such as Denmark.

In Belgium, the amount of the pension is related to the duration of the career and the remuneration received. If the career has been short and the earnings low — which is very often the case with women and other atypical workers — the pension will be very small.

In Luxembourg, the amount of the pension is related to the length of the insured career, and the earnings received. If the career has been short and the earnings low, the pension will be very small. Workers who "carry on a very limited salaried activity", such as teachers, who work for 11 hours per week in secondary education and 12 hours per week in primary education, are not entitled to a pension.

As already mentioned, the social security systems of certain countries provide a social pension which is not linked to work. One may cite the example of Denmark, where the institution of pension rights is based on periods of residence in Denmark, independently of whether the person has worked under a typical or atypical contract of employment. The same applies to the Netherlands. Pensions, which are of the same amount for everybody, are financed from public funds. There is also a legal pension system, the "supplementary workforce fund", which grants a pension in proportion to the total contributions paid, which are in turn related to working time. Part-time workers receive a supplementary pension, the amount of which varies in proportion to their contributions. Those who work less than 10 hours per week are, however, excluded from this pension, the amount of which is in any case modest, as it does not come to even 10% of the old age pension.

The arrangements in Ireland are similar to the Danish system. All people are entitled to receive an old age pension from the age of 66.

COMPLEMENTARY SYSTEMS GENERALLY EXCLUDE WORKERS UNDER NEW FORMS OF EMPLOYMENT: STEPS TOWARDS EXTENDING THEM

As a rule, occupational social security systems do not integrate atypical jobs. Now, this is a violation of the principle of equality which has received attention in recent years in relation to part-time working. Certain judgements issued by national courts and by the Court of Justice, as well as the Council Directive on the implementation of the principle of equal treatment for men and women in occupational social security systems, are in favour of extending the complementary system to part-time workers.

In the Federal Republic of Germany, as part-time working and non-permanent employment are not taken into account in the legal provisions, the question had arisen as to whether part-time working could be integrated into the complementary retirement system within the framework of companies. If part-time workers are excluded in general, this constitutes, according to the German Federal Court (judgement of 6 April 1982) a violation of the general principle of equality. By itself, the difference in the duration of working between, in particular, full-time and part-time working is not sufficient to justify exclusion.[16] Moreover, the Court of Justice of the European Communities, in one of its most recent judgements issued on 13 May 1986 (aff. 170/84), has explicitly declared that benefits granted to workers under the terms of a company pension scheme are an advantage coming under the application of the provisions of the treaty which call for equality of treatment (article 119). This ruling expresses the spirit and objective of the draft directive on equal treatment for men and women in occupational social security systems, already mentioned, which was approved by the Council of Social Affairs Ministers at the beginning of June 1986.[17] Our view is that this directive — the future of which is admittedly uncertain — opens the legal path which will lead to equal treatment for non-permanent workers. Its positive message for atypical workers' social security status remains, although the national protection and social security systems are still far from recognising their specific problems.

---

16. It should be pointed out that in many texts of collective agreements concerning part-time workers one finds clauses extending this benefit to this category of workers. See also the Model Union Agreement for Part-Time Workers drawn up by the Irish Congress of Trade Unions (ICTU).

17. See text of directive, published in OJ no. L225/40 of 12.8.86.

AFFILIATION AND CONTRIBUTION CONDITIONS FOR THE WORKERS INVOLVED: THE SOURCE OF INFERIORITY AND INEQUALITY

Atypical employees are not in a position to fulfil the minimum requirements for affiliation and prior contributions during the reference period which all social security systems finally specify. Under these conditions, there is a diminution in rights, particularly to an unemployment allowance, but also to an illness allowance, a maternity allowance (depending on the country), a disability allowance, as well as the right to a retirement pension. As benefits are generally calculated on the basis of salary received, the benefits received by atypical employees are necessarily smaller than those paid to typical workers. One cannot avoid concluding that even the affiliation and contribution conditions imposed on atypical workers constitute a source of inferiority. These conditions are a cause of inequality, although national laws often mention the principle of equality. But as the factual reality is quite different, this principle is to a certain extent devoid of content.

THE PROTECTION GIVEN BY SOCIAL SECURITY TO WORKERS UNDER NEW FORMS OF EMPLOYMENT IS INADEQUATE

Not all atypical employees receive the same protection, of course. A worker employed half-time on a permanent basis is entitled to more protection than another worker who is also part-time but employed for three hours per day, or intermittent or temporary workers, to say nothing of occasional workers.

If the general rule is that atypical employees are generally less protected than traditional workers, who always provide the model for social security regulations, it is equally true that certain groups of atypical workers enjoy a very small and inadequate degree of protection. We have already seen that when atypical employees do not succeed in meeting the required conditions — and without regard to their wish to work — the amount of benefits allocated (for example, unemployment, pension, maternity or family allowance) will be very small.

It also happens that certain workers have to pay their social security contributions — and do so — but do not meet all the conditions required in order to be entitled to the minimum level of benefit (or at least some benefits, according to the country: family, disability, unemployment allowances). This is the case, for example, in Belgium where a worker, to be able to avail of social security benefits, must have worked for at least three hours per day during the reference period. If the worker has worked less than three hours, then those days are not taken into consideration for certain benefits granted by the social security system, even when these social security contributions have been paid.

This was also the typical (and traditional) position for women who had worked more or less continuously in industry, with several interruptions due to family life, and who never managed to meet the conditions entitling them to a satisfactory or even an unsatisfactory pension.

It is still the position for a large number of non-permanent male workers (teachers, artists) whose contributions are paid every time that they manage to get a job, but who lose their rights to benefits, because they are not able to work for long enough to satisfy the legal requirements.

In certain countries there are some workers who cannot reach the threshold demanded by the social security system because either the number of hours worked — which differs from one country to another — or else the amount of their earnings is not sufficient. These workers are excluded from social security. It may be envisaged here that the present unemployment situation may bring about a rise in the number of workers who, while working say for 17 hours (rather than 18) per week, are deprived of all social security cover. There are also home-based workers who, in many countries, do not fulfil the criteria of social security liability. In Belgium for example, home-based workers, in order to qualify for social security, must come within a legal definition which covers only craft workers, the original home-based workers, while it does not include home-based intellectual workers and teleworkers.

A large number of employees are driven in the direction of ''self-employment'', though continuing to work in conditions of subordination after having achieved their new classification, so that their employer can get out of his or her obligations in relation to the social security system by appealing to the competitiveness or even the survival of the company. One therefore cannot avoid asking questions as to the adequacy of the protection given by the national social security systems to their atypical workers.

PUBLIC AUTHORITIES FAVOUR CERTAIN NEW FORMS OF WORK BY EXEMPTING A COMPANY FROM ITS SOCIAL CONTRIBUTIONS

Another striking feature which has already been observed in all member countries is that the public authorities are favouring certain new forms of work by exempting them from payment of social contributions. These contributions are paid partly or even totally by the State. Basically, this is a policy expressed through practical legal measures which particularly encourage non-permanent employment. This is the case, for example, with early retirement, an institution which is found in almost all member states (for example Spain, Belgium, Italy, France, the Federal Republic of Germany, the United Kingdom, the Netherlands, and it is also being proposed in Greece in a very recent law). The same is true of the contracts designed for young people (and in fact for older people who come under the influence of the regulations): the training contract, the educational contract, the apprenticeship contract, depending on the country. The most striking case is Italy, where the employment/training contract — set up by the 1984 law, which relieves the employer of (among other things) social security obligations — has been an unprecedented success. The employer pays, as salary costs, a very modest charge which was set for apprentices (2500 lire per week), while the rate of contribution in this category for employees under new forms of work contract is the same as for typical employees; it comes to about 9% of their remuneration. A considerable proportion of young workers, we know, comes into the labour market — even if only provisionally — by this path preferred by the employers.

The same applies in France to young employees working in the category of "odd jobs". This is also the case when an employer takes on an unemployed person who has been registered as unemployed for a certain length of time: the unemployed person continues to be insured by the State and not by the employer. We have already seen that recent legislative measures in Belgium provide for State intervention to pay social contributions, instead of the employer, where a youth contract or early retirement deals are involved.[18] It is clear, however, that these State interventions in the social security area — which also appear in the form of invalidity retirement and technical unemployment allowances — have the following effects:

— firstly, they pass on to the general public a cost which ought to

18. See Chapter II.

be paid by companies (i.e. employers), — a measure which does not ease the problems of financing the social security systems;

— secondly, they favour certain new forms of work, without offering them the corresponding protection.

These measures seem rather to introduce inequalities; they are short-term policies and provisions in relation to the phenomenon of atypical employment, and especially non-permanent employment, which deserves a completely different level of attention and a different policy treatment.

A LARGE NUMBER OF WORKERS UNDER NEW FORMS ARE BORDERING ON OR INDEED JOINING THE "NEW POOR"

It has become clear that a large number of people working under an atypical form of employment, even if they are doing so with an employment contract which is not too far removed from a typical contract, are inadequately covered by social security. But there are also many atypical employees who are not covered by social security or social assistance at all. The most disadvantaged atypical workers belong to the "minorities" of women, young people and redundant older workers who do not have a stable income (pension) and work on "odd jobs" while remaining unemployed for long periods. Researches carried out in Belgium have shown that the stereotype of the poor person has altered radically as far as age is concerned: more and more young people are fitting the description.[19]

This category, which constitutes a considerable band of the "new poverty", with all the problems of the new poor — social exclusion, possible psychological problems, anti-work attitude — is frequently joined by non-permanent workers, employed on a regular basis rather than occasionally like those previously mentioned, who do not succeed in finding a new job quickly. Even if this group is covered by social security, the protection and rights deriving from such coverage last only for a short time, especially in view of the measures most recently taken by governments who, appealing to the general crisis, have placed limits on protection and rights (time-limits: for example the duration of unemployment allowances). The systems of assistance, moreover, where they exist, even if they have not been affected by the economic crisis, have not been designed to deal with

19. See *Revue Belge de sécurité sociale*, 1986, no.4-5.

lifelong occupational instability for a growing number of workers. These systems of social security and social assistance, given the way in which they work, do not seem suited, in an overall sense, to cope with the problems of providing social protection for atypical employees.

THE NEED: SOCIAL SECURITY LAW SHOULD ADJUST ITS PARAMETERS TO THE NEW SOCIAL RISKS: LIFE "WITHOUT MUCH WORK" OR CHRONIC UNEMPLOYMENT

A large number of atypical workers, given the new logic of the labour market (i.e. the new company policy of employing the workers in the hard core on a permanent basis, and temporary workers on fixed-term, part-time contracts), are now destined to be marginalised and thus consigned to the ranks of the new poor. If they have a precarious position, their career prospects are those of the non-typical subordinate worker: they need a different kind of social protection. Social security law, with its multiple variants from country to country, needs to be readjusted. To the extent that atypical employment is not a phenomenon confined to a particular historical context, but rather arises from a restructuring of the labour market following economic changes and government and employer policies, and to the extent that it brings new social risks (more precisely, risks that are not new, but that are now appearing under new forms, such as periods of inactivity during the worker's active career, considered not as an exceptional but as a normal phenomenon), these risks should be taken on by the public purse following appropriate changes in the provisions of social security law[20] with regard to the new employment-related risks which call for a differentiated treatment of unemployment. The legal resources needed to meet this need are not the same, and form part of the social security system.

Certain tendencies, such as the uncoupling of some benefits from an occupational activity — for example, maternity and family allowances — which has already been achieved in certain member states, would, if they emerged as strongly in other member states, have a positive effect on the social protection of the atypical employee.

---

20. In the Community context, an attempt must be made to deal with the problems thus caused by atypical employment for the social security system, in a much faster timescale than that proposed by the OECD in *Dépenses Sociales 1960-1990: Problèmes de croissance et de maîtrise*, Paris, 1985.

The establishment of a guaranteed minimum social income would appear, moreover, to be an absolutely indispensable step in dealing with the problems of unemployed people without a prospect of rapidly securing a new job, and with the problems of the new poor. It could serve as a social safety-net offering protection against social exclusion (social dualism). A guaranteed minimum social income already exists in some countries, while in others one may see a move in that direction. But the allocations of social assistance in this direction are incomplete, leaving room for interruption and not answering the needs of situations linked to long-term unemployment, especially among young workers. However, a guaranteed minimum social income would not seem to offer a sufficient means of protection for all categories of atypical employees, especially those with a regular succession of periods of activity and periods of inactivity. In this case, special provisions are needed, designed to cover these new risks. The current inadequacies in the social security rules leave a lot of elbow-room for insurance companies who may number certain groups of atypical employees among their clients. In this connection, the problem of privatising the social security system arises: would this be acceptable in the twelve countries of the European Community, to the detriment of social protection as this concept is generally understood in Europe?[21]

It seems relevant to recall here the demand for a minimum wage for housewives (although this group cannot be included among atypical employees) which seems closely related to the call for a guaranteed minimum social income. And indeed it is closely related to that demand as far as its function is concerned, the difference being that in the second case one is dealing with a wage for unpaid work carried on within the family.[22] The principal argument advanced by its proponents is that, since the organisation of the economy is based on the unpaid work performed by women within the family — a contribution ignored by all economists, including Marxists — this work should be recognised and housewives should be paid a minimum

---

21. See Institut Européen de Sécurité Sociale, "Privatisation et Sécurité Sociale", report to the Commission (Prof. J. van Langendock), Louvain, October 1986.

22. See in this context the European Parliament document (1984) on the social and economic content of housework. The defenders of the idea of a minimum wage for housewives demand its payment for at least a transitional period, the indispensable period to allow all women to get ready for active life in the trading sector. This proposal is made to counter the basic argument of women who indignantly refuse this "remuneration", on the grounds that it would consolidate the thankless position of housewives who, largely because they are shut up within the family home, are unable to enrich their personalities, gain new experiences and achieve personal development through the work which they do.

wage. In this way, both their economic[23] and social[24] functions would be recognised.

There is undoubtedly a need for specific proposals on social security and protection for atypical employees. How should the machinery for compensating unemployment be adapted to atypical employment, or by what other means should one cover long periods of unemployment, or successive sequences of employment and unemployment, during an entire professional career? Can one put forward, as an "emergency measure" for countries in the group including the United Kingdom, Ireland and Denmark, the introduction of flexible conditions for social contributions which would make it possible, on the principle of analogy, to grant comparable benefits to atypical workers? And might one propose for other countries, such as the Federal Republic of Germany, Belgium or Greece (provisionally, among others), that they should undertake a broader interpretation of the conditions required for the payment of benefits, which would have the effect of favouring the rights of atypical employees within the framework of the social security system?

It should be pointed out that in Luxembourg the very recent reform of the unemployment and compensation fund (through a law passed on 29 April 1987) is associated with a more modern understanding of the relationship between employment and unemployment. The fund will henceforth be known as the "Employment Fund", and includes a special section designed to encourage the training, hiring and re-hiring of job seekers.

It would be a good idea to undertake research projects with several objectives in the social security area. A detailed investigation of the impact of new forms of work on social security law, and the new social needs, could be carried out by specialists in the social security field. One aim would be to identify the possibilities of adapting the rules of social security and social protection generally, in accordance with the legal characteristics of each country's system, the complexity and extreme technicality of which are well known. Another aim would be to bring out the contradictions which exist between the ethos of social security law in the Community's member states — their fully European spirit which contrasts sharply with the ethos permeating social protection schemes for workers on other continents — and the

---

23. In Italy, some feminist organisations have proposed that the conditions of housework should be regulated (timetable, minimum pay, health conditions) through collective bargaining at national level, on the model of the negotiations carried on by workers in the formal trading sector of the economy.

24. In the same country, on the identity cards of housewives, the words "nulla facente" are entered under the heading "occupation".

"damage" which this method has been sustaining on account of the development of atypical forms of employment which have yet to be taken on board. One is aware, of course, that very substantial problems of a financial nature — sometimes, it is said, extremely serious problems — arise in connection with the social security system, and these must not be brushed aside.[25] What is being suggested here is an exploration of the domain of the law and its possibilities, with regard to the social protection of so-called atypical employment; attention should be paid to the atypical workers and their rights — not the right of the poor to receive social assistance, but the worker's right to social insurance.[26]

In any case, the problems posed for the social security system by atypical employment have already been pointed out, without any need to refer to the explosion of the new typology of employment contracts and new forms of employment in general.[27] These are current problems — with future implications — arising from the current organisation of work in what is known as post-industrial society, an area which includes the member countries of the European Community. These countries are carrying their past along with them, together with the "lessons" of one hundred years of social insurance which have shaped the social security system. Just as we cannot abandon our European heritage of "one hundred years of social insurance", so also we have a duty to adapt this heritage to meet the challenge of atypical employment, while maintaining its spirit of social integration — although it was this that first revealed the limitations of social insurance and is now driving us towards "a search for a new balance of the techniques used by the social security system, in the context of the rationalisation of that institution, which today is indispensable".[28/29]

---

25. This question is receiving attention in France at the moment. See Le Monde, 26 May 1987, especially the articles by J.-J. Dupeyroux, "Néolithique", and C.J. Allègre, "Les experts et la démocratie".

26. See Guy Perrin, "La reconnaissance du droit à la protection sociale comme droit de l'homme", Travail et Société, vol.10 no.2, May 1985, pp. 255 ff.

27. See for example Guy Perrin, "Cent ans d'assurance sociale", Travail et Société, vol.2 nos. 2,3 and 4, June-December 1984, pp. 195-208, 319-330, 412-433; by the same author, "L'avenir de la protection sociale dans les pays industriels: crises, défis et mutation des valeurs", Les Futuribles, October-November 1985, pp. 28-52, and the bibliography cited; ILO, La Sécurité Sociale à l'horizon 2000, Geneva, 1984.

28. Guy Perrin, "Cent ans ... ", loc. cit., p. 431.

29. See also the following observations by the same author: "Reform of the social security system is such an urgent necessity that it is already going on, if not always in the texts of laws, then at least in the minds of those concerned. In order to be useful and acceptable, it must be designed as a safeguarding of the salient values of the institution, not as the sign for dismantling the social protection system under the weight of its own crises or

the economic crisis. Even if it is not approached globally and systematically — which very few countries dare to do — the reform of the social security system would still benefit by being placed in an overall perspective and a forward-looking framework which include the stages of a process orientated not merely towards the solution of present difficulties, but more importantly towards meeting future needs. To this end, it is worth distinguishing between the following types of question: immediate problems of reallocation and finance, which can be solved by rationalising systems; medium-term challenges, especially of an economic and demographic kind, which need to be taken up as quickly as possible; and finally the problem of adapting continually to shifts in society's values. This voluntary and constructive adaptation process is doubly effective, because it can match and balance the development of social mores during the phase of transition towards a new type of society.''

V
THE USE OF COLLECTIVE BARGAINING: NEW PERSPECTIVES AND LIMITATIONS

Since the first appearance of new forms of work in various member states, collective bargaining has been effectively used, as we have seen (although in different ways depending on the country), in order to secure greater flexibility in the rules on employment relationships, adapting them to the new needs of companies.[1] The trade union organisations were generally taken by surprise during the first stage of the process — a stage which went on for quite some time — and found themselves to a certain extent being "dragged along" at the negotiating table. They were not always equipped with clear and systematic proposals, and this was in sharp contrast to the wide range of proposals and solutions advanced by the employer organisations.[2]

However, after this shaky start, the trade union organisations made up for lost ground and began redefining, along with their overall policies,[3] the strategy to be followed in connection with new forms of work.[4] The state of "immobility" has been either completely

---

1. G. Lyon-Caen, "La bataille truquée de la flexibilité", *Droit Social*, December 1985, p. 801.

2. It must be said that the behaviour and proposals emanating from the trade union organisations, as these have appeared during negotiations touching on new forms of work — whether or not these have been successful — vary considerably from one country to another. But they often vary as well within a single country; here one may mention the case of France, and also Italy. Taken by surprise at the beginning, the unions were not able to develop systematic alternative proposals at once, whereas on the employer side of the table there was a veritable flowering of "creative imagination" on the subject of adaptability: it was the employer spokespersons who were laying down the ground-rules for the contest. On the aim of the negotiations to be carried on with the European trade unions as seen from the employers' point of view, see J.J. Oechslin, "Travail et flexibilité: le point de vue des employeurs", *BIS*, 2/85, pp. 203-205.

3. See G. Spyropoulos, "Le rôle des syndicats dans un monde en mutation", loc. cit., pp. 3 ff.; see also Edmond Maire, "Les défis lancés au syndicalisme", *BIS*, 3/4 1985, pp. 399 ff.; by the same author, "Quelques jalons pour l'avenir du syndicalisme", *Travail et Société*, 1986, pp. 103 ff.; and Mathias Hinterscheid, "Le rôle du travail, des travailleurs et de leurs syndicats dans la société de demain (principal themes proposed for the general report of the 5th CES statutory congress, Milan, 13-17 May 1985), *BIS*, 1/1986, p. 14.

4. At European level, the CES is also preparing its strategy in favour of new forms of work and new rights for workers with an "atypical" employment relationship; see Mathias Hinterscheid's comment: "The trade union movement intends to fight . . . for the defence of important social advances, and the creation of new rights which are suited in a positive way to the new forms of work". He envisages "the inclusion within union activities of

overturned or else is well on the way to extinction, depending on the country involved.

Collective bargaining has often followed the traditional, well-worn channels, but at the same time it has opened new channels. These new channels have revalued the negotiating process, while at the same time establishing a new relationship between legal rules and rules established by agreement. Here, the question of the hierarchy of sources arises. Recent developments have given collective bargaining a new face and new purpose. Its development may mark a turning-point in employment relationships within Community member states.

TRADITIONAL CHANNELS AND NEW CHANNELS

The most important new channels are those which have caused the emergence of "little by little" collective bargaining. Negotiations have developed according to the particular bargaining conditions of each country. The heterogeneous nature of their occupational relationships means that the emphasis is placed sometimes on sectoral bargaining and sometimes on company-level bargaining, while the posture adopted by the State varies: sometimes it maintains a discreet presence at the negotiating table, sometimes it intervenes openly, while in other cases it leaves the bargaining process entirely to the social partners.[5]

The channel of collective bargaining at national level — in its classic framework although in a new context — has been effectively followed in Belgium. It started with the signature of the intersectoral collective agreement of 13 February 1981 on the duration of employment;[6] others followed, including the "Hanssens" experiment. In Spain, despite the achievements of collective bargaining in the matter of tripartite national agreements, notably in 1981, 1982 and 1984, the law alone has taken on the reforms connected with new forms of work. In Italy, on the other hand, there are negotiations on new forms of work, and even a new style of proceeding. The State does not merely set up the framework for negotiations, encourage those negotiations, and put its official signature on the resulting agreement; it does more

those workers having the weakest connections with the company, for example those with non-permanent positions, those in subcontracting companies, home-based workers, part-time workers", loc. cit., pp. 14-15.

5. See Boyer, "La flexibilité du travail en Europe", loc. cit., pp. 20 ff.

6. See E. Vogel Polsky, "Crise, maintien de l'emploi et partage du travail", Geneva colloquium, loc. cit., pp. 80 ff.

than that, actually participating in the bargaining process as a private party. It signs the collective agreement as a third party on an equal footing with the other two. The novelty of this new-style collective agreement lies partly in the fact that it sets maximum levels, whereas previously minimum levels were set. The principle is that things which have been dealt with at national level are not renegotiable at company level. The new channel of negotiation works through a system of tripartite national agreement. The first collective agreement, the celebrated "Scotti agreement" of 1983, was signed by all the trade union organisations.[7] During the second phase of this period, however, the majority of the CGIL union confederation decided that it could not sign the 1985 protocol, as it did not agree with the idea of centralised tripartite negotiations.[8] The fact that the protocol was signed by the other two main confederations made it possible for the Socialist-led Italian government to issue a decree which incorporated its essential content. That decree led to greater flexibility in conditions of recruitment and in the regulation of part-time working. In Italy, the preferred name for this sort of legislation is "negotiated laws".[9]

In France also, during the course of 1984, a very broad collective bargaining process was undertaken between the two main employer federations and the trade union organisations. The aim was, by making certain concessions, to allow companies to be dispensed from certain compulsory regulations laid down by labour law, concerning, among other things, certain new forms of work: the fixed-term contract, temporary employment, and part-time working. The negotiations went ahead with implicit government backing, and a protocol was in fact signed, but these negotiations did not lead to

---

7. These comprise the Confederazione Italiana Sindacati Lavoratori (CISL, which has a Christian Democrat majority of 60-70%, and a Socialist minority); the Unione Italiana del Lavoro (UIL, which contains 55% Socialists and the rest Republicans and Social Democrats); and the Confederazione Generale Italiana del Lavoro (CGIL, which is predominantly Communist).

8. The CGIL had suggested adjustments in the system of industrial relations, to face up to the realities of the 1980s, on two levels of bargaining: the sectoral level and the company level. The confederation's position was that the tripartite national negotiations should deal with measures to be taken in order to combat unemployment, or to modify the tax or social security system; but they believed that indexation should only be discussed between employers and employees.

9. Given the importance assumed by bargaining at this level, one might consider recalling the analysis put forward by M. Aglietta, which may have implications for Europe in general. Among other things, he writes that "collective bargaining, even if it preserves its legal independence, will be increasingly subject to an overall incomes policy imposed in an authoritarian fashion by the State" (p. 329). However, not only salaries are involved; the overall policy also concerns employment. The State, in any event, cannot avoid having this protagonist's role: "The State, because it sums up all social norms, becomes a totaliser of tensions" (p. ii). See M. Aglietta, *Régulation et crise du capitalisme. L'expérience des Etats-Unis*, Calmann-Lévy, 1986.

a collective agreement, because they came up against stiff opposition from the lower echelons of the trade union organisations. These abortive discussions had, however, prepared the ground for legislative intervention.[10]

At sectoral level, collective bargaining on new forms of work is beginning to make space for itself, although it is developing in a selective and undoubtedly non-egalitarian manner: one finds collective agreements at this level in the Federal Republic of Germany, the United Kingdom, Ireland and elsewhere. In France, as already noted, temporary workers represent a separate sector of activity, with its own collective agreement. In Belgium and the Netherlands, also, temporary workers have their own collective agreement.

It is, however, at company level that most negotiations in favour of new forms of work take place, and this is true of all member states, with the exception of Greece, Portugal and Denmark, where the new forms have not yet been made the subject of special regulations. Employer organisations encourage collective agreements at this level and do their best to secure them, whereas the unions prefer collective agreements to be made at sectoral level. But they are often forced — sometimes by the sheer pressure of circumstances — to conclude agreements at this level, even though they have to make concessions in the face of enormous difficulties with employment: company employees themselves willingly accept diminutions of the rights which they have achieved, so as to keep their jobs. This "docility" among the workforce is partly explained in other countries by the weakness, and sometimes the non-existence, of company trade union organisations, which are replaced by other representative bodies. In such cases, as the unions cannot become involved in "concession bargaining" — prevented by their principles, but perhaps also by the lack of an updated strategy — the employers often prefer to deal with company commitees or works councils. This happens, of course, in countries where there are two bodies for representing employees: in France, for example, or in the Federal Republic of Germany. Sometimes, in other places, new unions emerge, such as the autonomous unions in Italy, which are clearly separated from the classic trade union organisations which act at national level.

Company agreements incorporate and express all sorts of "rules for adaptation". If one could generalise one would say that, on the

---

10. G. Bellier, "Après l'échec des négociations sur la flexibilité", *Droit Social*, 1985, pp. 79 ff.; R. Soubie, "Après les négociations sur la flexibilité", *Droit Social*, loc. cit., pp. 95 ff, pp. 221 ff. Despite the fact that the outcomes of these negotiations go in opposite directions, one can discern parallels between the two approaches, the Italian and the French.

one hand, company agreements are striking on account of their "creative" provisions in favour of new forms of work. On the other hand, one notices that instead of conferring rights and advantages on employees, they take them away. They have often encouraged an uncontrolled spread of atypical employment, without gaining anything for the workers in general. Although this varies from one country to another, depending on the power of the trade union organisations, there is no doubt that many provisions in collective agreements concerning new forms of work are contrary to some legal provisions, and even contrary sometimes to certain general principles of labour law.

THE PROBLEM OF THE HIERARCHY OF SOURCES

In the majority of member states, especially the Continental ones, the idea has always prevailed that the law, being the primary source of labour law in countries following the conventions of Civil Law, has got to guarantee all workers a minimum level of protection, below which collective agreements cannot be permitted to go.[11] A collective agreement can, however, derogate from the law *in melius* — in a direction more favourable to the workers. This principle was (and still is) written into various legal texts in those countries; it is indeed at the basis of "public social policy". However, in the new economic context, with agreements covering the new forms and creating obligations for workers which are not laid down by law, new problems have arisen. It was felt that legally-based regulations had become too inflexible and constraining for companies, whose agreements, appealing to the danger of dismissal, have often derogated from the law through negotiation, and adopted provisions which are less advantageous to the workers. As labour law has to make its assessments according to these economic "constraints", it finds itself having to tolerate solutions which are far removed from the traditional image of labour law, as in the case of the hierarchy of sources.

The laws of several member states have to deal with delicate questions as to whether collective agreements can derogate *in pejus* (i.e. for the worse) from legal provisions, and to what extent they can undermine the minimum protection which they provide. There

---

11. See N. Aliprantis, "La place de la négociation collective dans la hiérarchie des normes", Paris, LGDJ, 1980.

is no doubt that the relationship between norms established by agreement and norms established by law is undergoing a process of redefinition.

In Italy, for example, having regard to recent developments, there is a change in the concept and function of collective bargaining. Parliament is passing laws which allow collective agreements to give relief from protective provisions in the law, or not to derogate *in melius* from the legal provisions. Case-law recognises that a collective agreement can have less favourable clauses than those envisaged by previous collective agreements.[12]

The development has been different, however, in the Federal Republic of Germany, where the legal system has for quite a long time allowed unions to derogate from the law through collective agreements, in both directions: for the better or for the worse. But the German unions have been unwilling to use this faculty of derogation to the detriment of wage-earners. Works councils (which are formally separate from the trade union organisations) have, on the other hand, been ready to take this path in recent years, in the context of "the crisis". But the Federal Labour Tribunal — which is contributing enormously to the development of labour law through case-law — has been forbidding this derogation in the "Betriebsvereinbarung" for the past twenty years. For a long time too, the case-law of the same court has held that there is no validity in company agreements which call into question the advantages stipulated in the individual employment contract. As these questions have been raised and debated in recent years, a recent decision of the Federal Tribunal (16 September 1986), while going in the same direction, clarifies and specifies the circumstances in which a works council can deal with workers' rights through negotiation. The essence of this decision is that the works council and the employer may not conclude company agreements except insofar as such agreements do not generally disimprove the situation of the workers in the establishment which they cover. As a general disimprovement in working conditions is forbidden, the only elements that can be modified through these negotiations are some principles for the distribution of premium payments, and various advantages, or bringing outdated regulations up to date: the company agreement cannot henceforth be used as an instrument for disimproving the rights of workers laid down in a collective agreement, i.e. agreed with the unions at a higher level.

---

12. G. Giugni, "Les tendances récentes de la négociation collective en Italie", *Revue Internationale du Travail*, 1984, pp. 643 ff.

As regards France,[13] it must be remembered that in 1982 legislation had envisaged the possibility of using an agreement to derogate from rules relating to the duration of employment, and timetables, while at the same time imposing special requirements as regards the representative nature of the bodies signing such agreements. Negotiations on, among other things, differentiated employment which have not led to agreements came under the same logic: derogation from certain compulsory rules of the labour code through collective agreements made at sectoral or company level. This possibility was opened up by the 1986 laws.

The "revaluation" of the collective agreement in relation to the law, which is common to almost all the Continental member states, does not yet mean that the problems arising as regards the hierarchy of sources have been solved.

The idea of a collective agreement more favourable to employees expresses a value of industrial culture which cannot permit an unlimited derogation *in pejus*: in such cases, how can one determine its relationship with the law and the individual employment contract? What is the "most favourable" content in the new state of affairs? It is now known that we have no guarantee that the collective agreement, as a source of norms imposed on the individual contract, will always continue to be more favourable and "preferable a priori" for employees at the present time.[14] What, then, is the new hierarchy of norms which is emerging, and what can we define as the content of its criteria?

As collective agreements do not lend themselves any less than legislative action to the adaptation of provisions to economic realities, one cannot avoid asking how far they extend. Where is the "hard core" of labour law which they cannot touch, and where is the sphere of action for the trade union organisations (and employer organisations) in the process of adapting or transforming labour law?

A NEW STAGE

There is no doubt that the role of collective bargaining is changing in almost all countries. It is not merely that a basic redistribution is going on — or in preparation, in some countries — between the role

---

13. X. Blanc-Jouvan, "Les développements récents de la négociation collective en France" (duplicated), Paris, 1986, pp. 18 ff.

14. See G. Lyon-Caen, "La bataille truquée", loc. cit., p. 808.

of labour law fixed by State legislation and the role of labour law forged by negotiation. What is equally important is that collective bargaining is acquiring a new content (function), is extending to other subjects, and is even tending to become "emancipated" in relation to the law. Its development is taking place in member states within a setting full of contradictions. Just as the power of the trade union organisations is receding in the great majority of countries, so at the same time there is a great surge in collective bargaining.

The essential aim of collective bargaining no longer seems to be remuneration, but rather employment, which includes the new forms of work. In reality, it seems that one can make out a sort of "displacement" of the field of negotiation in the majority of member states: forced into this area by the policy of squeezing or even freezing wages,[15] it is expanding especially on the side of employment and how it should be shared.[16]

Another feature is that collective bargaining seems to be entering a new phase of "exchange and counterbalance": the game is being carried on more and more within a new set of rules. This logic of exchange, by advantage and concession, seems to permeate all levels of negotiation — or at least to be tending in that direction. Not only does one increasingly find "little by little agreements" in the so-called central countries, but also the idea of exchange, of trade-off, is more or less apparent in certain key laws concerning new forms of work. Thus, while it is true that this new face of collective bargaining, after taking on board its "counterbalance" character, means that the resulting collective agreement is very close to collective agreements as known in the United States, what separates them, on the other hand, is precisely the importance which has always attached to legislation in the labour law of the majority of European Community member countries.[17]

The type of collective bargaining that has emerged in Italy — where the unions on the one hand are partly giving up their legal

---

15. This is the case in Greece at the moment, although in this country the aims of collective bargaining have always appeared too narrow; see among others Y. Kravaritou-Manitakis, "La Grèce", in A. Jammeaud and A. Lyon-Caen (eds.), *Droit du travail, démocratie et crise en Europe et aux Etats-Unis*, Actes Sud, 1986.

16. See X. Blanc-Jouvan, op. cit., p. 23; Boyer, loc. cit., pp. 369 ff. The same phenomena are found in the USA, where salary concessions sometimes reach half the agreed salary level.

17. One must always bear in mind the different position of collective agreements in the USA and Europe within the overall set of rules constituting labour law. However important the role of collective agreements in certain member countries may be, these are supported by a body of State legislation and their main concern is to improve on that legislation, although for some time they have been encroaching on its territory and aiming to modify it. Some shades of difference must of course be recognised in British and Irish law; but since joining the Community they are leaning somewhat in the Continental direction.

safeguards,[18] while on the other hand gaining some important advantages by way of counterbalance (such as the right to have a say in the fiscal and social policies of the State) — shows the new perspectives which can open up for bargaining and for organisations on both sides, particularly trade union organisations.[19]

These potentialities — not to say necessities — for collective bargaining and collective agreements in Europe[20] also underline the role which it has in the "reshaping" of labour law in the strict sense.

---

18. Moving from the well-known "garantismo" to a position of "controllo"; some people believe that this shows a new corporate state mentality in the Italian industrial relations system. On these developments see G. Giugni, "Il diritto del lavoro negli anni 80", *Giornale di diritto del lavoro e di relazioni industriali*, 1982, pp. 373 ff.; by the same author, *Prospettive del diritto del lavoro per gli anni 80*, 1983, pp. 3 ff., and "Les tendances récentes de la négociation collective en Italie", loc. cit.; T. Treu, "Recent development of Italian labour law", *Labour and Society*, January 1985, pp. 27 ff.

19. This can also be seen quite simply as an extension of "industrial democracy"; see R. Dahrendorf, *Classes et conflits de classes dans la société industrielle*, Paris, Mouton, 1972, pp. 259 ff. It is still true that the new forms of work oblige one to reflect not only on the development but also on the role of the trade union movement, and the role of the social function of business and the policies conducted by governments also. See G. Spyropoulos, loc. cit., p. 5.

20. See J.-C. Javillier, "Ordre juridique, relations professionnelles", loc. cit., p. 29. See also G.J. Bamber and R.D. Lansbury, "Industrial relations and technological change: towards a comparative technology?", report presented to the European Regional Congress of the International Industrial Relations Association, Vienna, 25-27 September 1984; and K. Tapiola, "La négociation, ce qu'elle peut et ne peut pas faire", *BIS*, 2/85, pp. 206-207.

VI
TENTATIVE CONCLUSIONS

The effects brought about by new forms of work as regards labour law and social security law in member states, although these are not the same everywhere, are creating new employment relationships in all countries, and throwing up new theoretical problems to be resolved. In general terms, it can be said that the new forms of work and activity have developed in a way which has created an imbalance between the protection of company rights and worker rights. They have threatened precisely the kind of traditional balance reflected by labour law — an institution, as specialists are well aware, that always takes some time to adapt to new situations.

1. *Negative effects, though of different dimensions according to the country.* It is true that in the first phase of their development, which has reached unexpected proportions, the effect of the new forms has been, generally speaking, rather negative: they have ignored certain basic principles and weakened the structure of labour law, causing it to be overtaken by "activity law", and depriving many workers under new forms of their social security entitlements. The two branches — labour law and social security law — have been seen as confined to workers with a typical employment relationship, enjoying stability and security of employment. Non-permanent workers under new forms of contract, in one way or another, partially or totally, have lain outside their ambit. The same has applied to salaried employees embarking on self-employment.

In certain countries these effects have been felt in a less dramatic fashion in relation to legal implications and changes in labour law. This is the case with the United Kingdom, Ireland and Denmark, but that is largely attributable to the particular nature of their labour law (Common Law, collective bargaining) rather than to the different impact of the new forms. The same holds true for Greece and Portugal, but in these two southern countries there is also the effect of a certain slowness and inflexibility which characterise their labour law. French, German, Italian and Spanish law — and the laws of Luxembourg too, though to a lesser extent — have shown a more dramatic reaction to the new forms: certain regulations are being introduced, although these are not always systematic or complete.

A new labour law is being explicitly formed to deal with the new range of employment contracts. However, it is a labour law which seems more like a law on company organisation than on worker protection. On the other hand, there are the beginnings of recognition for the ''new'' rights which are emerging as a trend towards the re-establishment of the lost balance.

2. *Towards a new classification: the two basic models.* The spread of new forms of work is leading to a new typology of employment contracts, which is now emerging and seems to follow two norms, two basic legal models of employment: on the one hand, the classic job with its traditional employment contract, and on the other hand, work under new forms with a very rich variety of configurations. Within the new range, one may draw a distinction between those jobs which may be termed employment without an employer — the status of the fake self-employed, subcontracting, possibly homeworking and teleworking, clandestine work in the grey or black economy — and the new forms under a non-permanent employment contract, notably the fixed-term contract, the temporary employment contract, the employment/training contract: it is in this type of contract that one finds the greatest lack of traditional guarantees, and this is the place where ''new'' rights and minimum standards are beginning to be defined — although this has not yet happened in all countries.

3. *Full integration and assimilation.* A comparative law survey can in no way propose a solution or common model. It is understood that each national system must find its own ways and work out its own techniques to integrate the new forms fully within its labour law and social security law.

However, as we find ourselves in the European Community area, which is characterised by a certain measure of homogeneity and a common understanding of these two branches of law, it is appropriate to offer some remarks of a general nature, which may eventually lead to an approach to the question of what conditions are required in order that the new forms may function in a positive manner. The essential condition would seem to be that they must be fully integrated and assimilated within labour law and social security law.

4. *A truly structural phenomenon; accepting it as such.* A systematic approach to the new forms of work, in a perspective of full integration by labour law and social security law, is made imperative by the realisation that this is no transitory phenomenon due to the current

crisis. The new forms express a truly structural phenomenon,[1] which is taking root and prefiguring the forms that work organisation may take after the year 2000. Therefore, they cannot be ignored, as they express not only this constraint imposed at the moment by company organisation, but also, in the future, needs for diversification and differentiation. It seems that there is a move towards a new definition of work, which may have nothing to do with under-employment. This new concept of work has to take account of the thousand faces of the question, the myriad individual special cases. It could be met by a succession of jobs rather than one stable job, or even by a multiplicity of jobs or occupations following individual preferences and personal needs.

In this perspective too, labour law and social security law obviously cannot continue to develop on the exclusive model of an employment relationship which is full-time and open-ended. While one is forced to accept the greater flexibility in the rules of work introduced by the new forms, this does not mean instant acceptance of cuts in the protection given by labour law and social security law. We should not penalise new forms of work which bring new flexibility to some inflexible arrangements, neither should we undermine legal protection: these are two separate issues and ought to be treated separately.

5. *Another definition of work: against all forms of segmentation.* Another factor militating in favour of full integration of the new forms of work within labour law and social security law is the following: it is not possible to perpetuate this split in the workforce between hard-core workers — already shrinking, and set to shrink still further in the future, even the immediate future — and peripheral workers. However, one is not dealing simply with "peripheral workers" linked to the company. There are people in this category who are not connected with any company, and whose working career is made up of active and inactive periods. There are "atypical" workers who move from one occupation to another, from one trade to another, and even workers who carry on two different trades at the same time: although the categories remain one-dimensional, the "subjects" filling them are becoming multi-skilled. The trend in our time is towards a multiplicity of jobs:[2] which other branches of the law, if not the

---

1. According to Boyer, this is probably a "new modification in the employer/employee relationship", loc. cit., p. 264.

2. See C. Tsoukalas, "Classes multidimensionnelles et 'sujets' polyvalents", loc. cit.

branches of labour law and social security law, will look after these workers under the system of new forms of work?

The new forms of work can only be accepted on the indispensable condition of equal status with typical employment. The imaginations of lawyers must produce solutions, both for labour law and for social security law, which could protect workers under new forms from the risk of impermanence. Labour law could, on the basis of a new definition of work, give non-permanent staff the rights enjoyed by typical employees: one can find already in national legislation certain paradigms of this form of assimilation (in the sense of equal treatment), but these are not enough.

6. *Emancipation through minimum levels of protection.* Only a minimum level of protection can contribute towards the emancipation of the new forms of work from their inferior status, and stop them developing in the direction that they are currently taking — partly influenced by their legal status — towards a lowering of standards in living and working conditions. Minimum guaranteed levels can allow new forms of work to be associated with skilled, well-paid jobs which advance one's career. Some experiments are moving in this direction, however limited (notably job-sharing). Only a basic level of protection can ensure that a choice of a new-style employment contract, for reasons of personal suitability, will not be penalised. In this way, it will be possible to secure respect for the new values related to work in general, expressed by the feminist and youth movements.[3] These movements have contributed towards an understanding that there are activities equivalent to employment even if they do not have a market value.[4] However, if these values are taken into account and put into practice by workers under new forms, without the existence of a guaranteed minimum level of protection, they will merely function as a trap, perpetuating the inferior status of the new forms of work. There is no doubt, in any event, that the emancipation of the new forms must include their defeminisation. One may already see a tiny trend in this direction, and positive prospects for the future: guaranteed minimum standards may prevent the extension of the legal status of traditional female work, which is an extremely weak one, to male work under new forms of contract.

7. *On the redefinition of the field of application of labour law and social security law.* To speak of redefining the field of application of these

---

3. See one of the articles inspired by these values: Patrick Boulte, ''Promouvoir la civilisation du temps choisie'', in *Pour une nouvelle politique sociale en Europe*, loc. cit., pp. 119 ff.

4. In any case, the social sciences are currently redefining the term ''work''.

two branches of law, or of their taking on board the new forms of work, comes to the same thing. Since the development of new forms of work has placed a large number of workers outside the umbrella of protection, thus depriving them of their rights, action is needed to offer them once again the protection of labour law and social security law. Of course action is needed in many member states. It is undoubtedly necessary to undertake legal reforms in certain states, or to complete them in other. Legal means to this end must be found. But sometimes there is a need, depending on the legal system involved, not to find legal means of taking on board the new forms of work — for example, by extending the concept of subordination — but rather, on the contrary, to find ways of preventing them from being placed outside the general field of application of labour law and social security law. This is what happens, for instance, with all the laws which deprive workers under new forms of employment of their social security rights by prolonging the minimum period required for entitlement to those rights. In reality, for these two branches of the law, it is very often a question not of extending into new territories but of recapturing lost territory, so that a minimum level of protection can be guaranteed for subordinate workers in a weak economic position — the group to which labour law and social security law historically owe their existence. Otherwise, one finds oneself faced with a paradox, namely, that labour law and social security law will be applied mostly to management staff, who are not in a weak economic (nor yet social) position, and who have been covered by the protection offered by labour law through a sort of process of osmosis (rather than, for example, through collective struggles).

The basic problem for labour law is, first of all, to regain its balance between protecting the interests of workers and protecting the interests of companies. More precisely, the aim is not to restore the lost balance just as it was — the new forms of work have already changed the landscape of labour law — but rather to re-establish a balance between the protection of worker and company interests. It is not a question of maintaining or restoring rules which are inflexible and therefore ineffectual. The challenge is to re-establish, in a certain way, the classic function of labour law in Europe, while accepting that it is an adaptable institution.

Employment is certainly developing in the same way in the various free-market countries, but that does not prevent labour law and the values of industrial relations, depending on social history and other circumstances, from being relatively different from one country to another, and from one continent to another. Despite a certain process of osmosis which influences, in particular, new forms of work, these cannot obliterate the industrial values which have shaped the labour law of member countries. A basic value, permeating labour law in all countries, is the concept of solidarity: in Japan, the place of this concept is taken by the principle of segmentation, which is at the same time a cultural value permeating Japanese labour law and labour relations. Another European principle, which works in the same way, is the principle of equality. Reforms relating to new forms of work must take account of that fact.

8. *The two methods of adaptation: the path of legislation and the path of agreement*. The relationship between labour law and the new forms of work is more complex than might be suggested by a simplistic image depicting, on the one hand, the new forms developing in a wild and uncontrolled manner, and on the other hand the labour and social security law which has to "civilise" these forms and bring them under its own control. Nevertheless, there is no doubt that labour law and social security law do have to intervene in order to guarantee minimum levels of protection to workers under new forms.

This legal action is necessary not only because it fills the gaps which exist in some countries where the law has not yet tackled the problem of the new forms, but also because in other countries the existing regulations are not always complete, while elsewhere they often need to be supplemented and improved, and certain rights — for example, collective rights — need to be restored to workers under new forms of employment.[5]

The two traditional paths towards this end are the path of legislation and the path of agreement, already used, as we have seen, in certain member states. A third way also seems to be opening up (at least it has been seen in Italy): the approach of "negotiated laws", the outcome of explicit transactional bargaining. This should be done with all trade union organisations.

Every country, of course, has its own preferred path for adapting labour law to recent developments. But if one wants to ask which of the two traditional paths seems more promising in guaranteeing minimum protection to workers under new forms of employment, the answer lies in the area of regulation by law. The reason for this is that the trade union organisations are not willing, in all countries, to agree to negotiate on protection lower than that which is laid down for workers under ordinary labour law. "Concession bargaining" has

---

5. See the Opinion of the Commission on internal and external adaptation of companies in relation to employment, Com.(87)229 *fine*, according to which the spread of new forms cannot take place without accompanying measures guaranteeing workers protection similar to workers under traditional employment contracts (17).

not become part of the practice of all trade union organisations in member countries, and in some of these it possibly will not be accepted for ideological reasons. In this case the most promising path, even for countries such as the United Kingdom or Ireland which give a prominent position to collective bargaining, would seem to be by means of legislation. It is self-evident that the path of collective bargaining — even in countries where the minimum protection of workers under new forms is ensured by law — can only work in conjunction with legislative action in order to secure the application or enhancement (or even the agreement) of minimum protection levels.

Although it is reasonable to consider here that the two traditional methods of adaptation ought to hold fast to what might be called the "fundamental social rights" of European workers, the content of this concept is not yet clear enough for it to be invoked. The rights involved do not derive exclusively from the employment relationship, and cover a whole range of social security benefits. But there is no doubt that any reform should be determined or defined by this minimum level. It would seem well worth while undertaking a research programme in this direction in member states, within the framework of the social cohesion to be achieved in the Community.

9. *The two main categories of workers under new forms: those excluded from protection.* A great number of workers will necessarily be left outside all protective coverage. Workers under new forms are divided, as we have seen, into two main categories. Firstly there are those who are employed with some kind of employment contract — fixed-term contract, temporary employment, etc. — who can benefit from minimum protection levels to the extent that the law guarantees this level, and gives them some legal status; this applies in some countries, but not all. Secondly, there are the workers under new forms who have no employment contract — the fake self-employed, clandestine workers, etc. — who cannot benefit from minimum protection within the framework of labour law: they do not come within its sphere of application, according to the established criteria.

While, traditionally, these categories of workers lie outside the application of protective application, we have seen the reasons advanced at the present time in favour of an extension of labour law in this direction: the idea is supported especially in Italy with regard to "parasubordinate" workers. However, even if a certain development of this kind did take place — for example, by enlarging the notion of subordination, which does not seem to be an immediate prospect — a large number of workers without contracts would still be untouched by any minimum protection.

One could nonetheless put forward the hypothesis that in countries where new forms of work have not yet received a definite legal status, their possible recognition could give minimum protection to workers moving out of the fake self-employed category or the black economy and into the category of workers employed under a new-style contract. In some countries such as Portugal — the same could be said of Greece — the ineffectiveness of labour law is blamed for the extension of black-market employment. The possible recognition of certain new forms could create an intermediate flexible status which could absorb a number of workers without a contract. But equally, one cannot rule out the inverse phenomenon: a shift in workers belonging to the ''hard core'' towards the category of workers in new forms (the non-permanent sector). Although it may be necessary, any initiative in favour of new forms must be taken with all the attention required by the balance that has to be maintained between economic and social considerations.

10. *Questions requiring further exploration*. During the present research project, certain questions have emerged which seem vitally important to the development of labour law — and social security law. Further exploration of these areas, within the perspective of ''normalising'' the new forms and making them work in a positive fashion, would appear very worthwhile.

a) *The renewal of the employment contract*. A question to be examined concerns the employment contract, which is once again a focus of theoretical interest, and is beginning to occupy an increasingly prominent position — as was formerly the case — within the discipline of labour law. As we have seen, the employment contract is becoming differentiated, it is frequently surrounded by formalities, and it provides minutely detailed definitions of its object (Chapter V, 3.4.2.). Along with this changing content it incorporates new functions, such as the training function. It is true that the employment contract can become an instrument of innovation, and contribute to the development of certain areas of labour law which it does not habitually treat (see R. Dahrendorf, ''Conflitto e contratto - relazioni industriali e comunità politica in tempo di crisi'', *Rivista di diritto del lavoro*, 1978, p. 223.). But how far can the free development of the wishes of all parties go in the framework of new kinds of contracts? The question arises, among other things, in connection with ''internal flexibility'', already discussed. This also affects the traditional employment contract, but has a major impact on new forms of work, which are based on needs for adaptability. "Internal flexibility" clauses — drawing their inspiration from the principles of Japanese employment contracts (but one must recall that lifetime contracts are the rule in that country) — may clash with legal provisions and with the cultural values, held in all Community countries, which assume for example that the employment contract fixes terms which cannot be changed unilaterally by the employer, on major questions such as the place of employment or the nature of work done. There is undoubtedly a need for flexibility, and there are legal provisions governing it. But the stability of the company's financial outcome, which new forms of work are set up to serve, cannot be used as a pretext for all kinds of instability in the employment contract.[6] While remaining open to innovation, the contract needs to set firm limits. Indeed the employment contract, in the light of the new forms which are developing, now appears a most interesting subject for research.

b) *The intervention of public authorities.* The involvement of public authorities in certain new-style employment contracts, as revealed by the present research project (Chapter V, 3.3., 3.4.3.1., and 4.7.), is another question deserving further study. Attention has already been drawn to employment/training contracts, contracts for job-sharing with an unemployed person, and early retirement contracts, with their variants from country to country. The public authorities aim to promote employment by means of these financial initiatives on behalf of the company, and social and sometimes fiscal concessions. One is forced to conclude that this constitutes a kind of encouragement to non-permanent employment. In Italy, this policy is also manifested through the fine which the employer must pay to the Unemployment Fund in cases of non-compliance with the collective agreement on part-time working; in any event, we are witnessing the evolution of a kind of labour law implying this type of intervention by the public authorities, with a logic which seems far removed from the protectionist spirit of traditional labour law. But perhaps it is too soon to explain the long-term incidence and objectives of these provisions. Do they amount to a ratification of a new concept of work? Can they offer — or provoke — some new guarantees to replace traditional

---

6. During some discussions it has even been suggested that the ideal type of employment contract would allow its conditions to be revised on a day-by-day basis! It is too soon to conclude that "workforce transfers between industrial groups undoubtedly prefigure an extension of socialisation in the use of the labour force", when these provisions are laid down in new-style contracts, i.e. those which institutionalise non-permanent working. See Boyer, loc. cit., pp. 237 and 374.

guarantees which are being lost? And a question of interest to those studying the role of the State in the development of industrial relations: how does one explain this type of active intervention on the part of the State at a time when the rhetoric of economic liberalism is winning the day and forbidding such interventions? Is this the State as "totaliser of tensions"? If so, what are the implications for a reshaping of relations with the "social partners"?

c) *Redefining the concept of subordination.* Another concept which needs to be worked out afresh is the notion of subordination, in its traditional sense, which lies at the very heart of labour law (Chapter V., 3.4.3.2.). The various procedures for exteriorising or delocalising work have led to a sort of fragmentation in the notion of subordination, or even a kind of apparent disappearance. We have seen how the criterion of subordination becomes hazy in the home-based working contract and the telework contract, and we have seen that the legal status of these forms of work is ambiguous in all member states (Chapter V, 2.3.). In Italy, especially, one is finding a broadening in the concept of subordination. But the trend towards changing the legal position of subordinate workers and making them into fake self-employed workers would require a revision of the traditional notion of subordination — and not just in Italy. Other criteria should perhaps be added, such as the criterion of organisation. Or else perhaps the traditional notion should be replaced by a whole set of notions, depending on the type of employment relationship involved. A whole new research field is opened up, which may provide us with tools for building a new balance and rendering unto Caesar (in this case, unto labour law) what is Caesar's.

d) *"Substitute" rights and new rights.* Attention has been drawn to the trend, found in national systems which have moved to regulate the new forms of work, towards recognising some "ersatz" (substitute) rights in connection with non-permanent jobs, such as end-of-contract compensation for fixed-term workers or temporary employees.

One may also note the emergence of some new rights, such as the right of part-time workers to priority of access to full-time employment in the companies where they are working (Belgium, Spain). The same is true of seniority rights: certain provisions state that the non-permanent worker who moves to a stable job does not lose seniority rights. These are undoubtedly pointers — beginnings of responses — to the "normalisation" of the new forms of work, and to some first, faltering, non-systematic steps which would repay further investigation.

The extension of collective rights to workers under new forms of employment may be seen in the same context. The road to be travelled in this case seems a long one: not all countries recognise such rights, and sometimes non-permanent staff are only recognised as having some of the collective rights (3.5.2.). The "threshold" problem often functions as a major stumbling-block to the recognition of either part-time or temporary employees — depending on the country — as being members of the company personnel. Certain national regulations have responded to this problem, even though their responses are sometimes dubious. The effect of imitation should work on the principle involved.

e) *Collective bargaining*. The role of collective bargaining in the transformation which is affecting labour law, on account of the extension of new forms, is another question which deserves systematic study. But the transformation of bargaining itself, and the transformation of collective agreements at all levels of negotiation, also deserve study. A problem which arises in some countries is the separation of the different levels of bargaining. How is bargaining defined as regards its highest level — inter-sectoral, national? Are general rules agreed at this level, as well as limits for negotiations at lower levels? The "turnaround" in the bargaining procedure, which has traditionally been a means of improvement, but is now also becoming an instrument of exchange and of reduced protection, demands, as we have seen, the preparation and acceptance of new ground-rules.

Research efforts may also be directed towards the question of the usefulness of collective bargaining in the context of an enlarged framework of co-operation, with a view to "social planning" involving not only workers under new forms of employment, with or without employment contracts, but also the new social minorities, the "new poor", as regards their employment problems.[7] This type of bargaining depends, of course, on the system of industrial relations in each individual country, but also on the ability of trade union organisations to represent not only the interests of the "new arrivals"

---

7. See Emilio Morgado Valenzuela, "Formas atipicas de trabajo y las relationes laborales", loc. cit., pp. 189 ff. See also the theses advanced by the European trade unions on negotiations about the new forms at the different levels at the European Trade Union Institute: *Flexibilité et emploi - Mythes et réalité*, op. cit., but compare also the debate between A. Gorz, P. Glotz and T. Fichter, "La plus grande liberté possible: Emancipation dans le travail", loc. cit., pp. 72, 77 and throughout as regards the possible new frontiers of bargaining.

in the trade union movement, but also of the "non-arrivals" (the unemployed, the new poor).

New forms in company-level negotiation could be a fascinating research topic. It is at this level that uncontrolled bargaining on new forms of work has been able to attack the "legal web" of protective rules which operate in two ways: protecting workers, but also protecting competition. In the development, or even the promotion, of new forms of work through bargaining, one cannot of course worry about the perpetuation of that traditional understanding of labour law in member states which also aims to avoid distorting competition. Companies — and national economies — whose competitiveness is to be based on new forms of work which permit unstable employment, badly protected, badly paid and consequently distorting competition, cannot be assured of a dynamic economic future. What place can they have in a Community which wants to remove all obstacles to competition?

EPILOGUE

That is what the workers and sculptors of Europe still don't know,
and it makes them sweat over a whole rock sometimes to no effect.
But there it is, a tricky thing, you've got to find the groove in the marble.

H. Michaux, *Au pays de la Magie*

To answer the general question raised at the Brussels colloquium as to the positive sides of the new forms of work: while they are good for company operations, the effects of the new forms on labour law and social security law have been pretty negative for the workers so far. Acting like a Trojan horse, the new forms have weakened labour law by undermining some of its general principles. They have also taken away, from workers under new forms of employment, the protection and advantages which employees with a typical employment relationship enjoy by virtue of labour law and social security law, both of which are built on the model of the typical employment relationship. In the present context of the Community, the development of new forms of work is creating a situation which often seems like a return to the early days of capitalism, when the trade unions were not yet fully formed and labour law was not yet organised. The new forms, however, contain a number of dynamic elements, and may prove positive on condition that they are fully taken on board by labour law and social security law. Their adaptability, the positive values which they are capable of generating, may contribute, on that indispensable condition, to the enhancement and effectiveness of legal regulations.

If they worked in the context of a general reduction in working time — as demanded by the trade unions — or even if they worked under current conditions to secure equal status with typical employment, the new forms would then be an effective means for the "improvement of living and working conditions". Detached from the protection given by labour law and social security law, however, they are liable to lead a large number of atypical employees into the path of unstable employment, with all that this entails, and even into the ranks of the new poor.[1]

---

1. In the current state of affairs, the new forms of work are certainly not going to lead people to the paths of heaven, "Aux Chemins du Paradis" — see the book of that title by André Gorz, published by Galileé, Paris, 1983.

The development of these new forms is weighing heavily on the development of labour law in member states in the decades leading up to the year 2000: labour law cannot afford either to disregard or to neglect these forms.

Labour law in Community member states — this cannot be said too often in connection with new forms of work — contrasts sharply with labour law on other continents. Its distinctive features mark the cultural landscape of Europe; it is a fundamental element in European industrial culture. To the degree that the protective functions of both labour law and social security law extend to all new forms of work, and to the degree that the principles of equality and non-discrimination are effectively applied to the new typology of employment relationships, these relationships will mark a new phase of labour law, continuous with the European tradition.

If the idea — or the strategy — is to avoid emphasising economic values at the expense of social values, then labour law and social security law, redefined in relation to the new realities on the basis of the strongly European principle of solidarity, could have many proposals to make on integrating new forms of work into the existing fabric. And collective bargaining at all levels — as well as those agents with collective autonomy — could have a major part to play in the renewal and redefinition of labour law.

BIBLIOGRAPHY

ALIPRANTIS Nikitas, [in Greek:] Part-time working in Greek law, *Law and Politics* review, 1982, p. 267.

BAKELS H.L., "Dutch Labour Law", in the *International Encyclopaedia for Labour Law and Industrial Relations*, edited by R. Blanpain, Kluver-Deventer, 1979.

BARBAGELATA H., "Different Categories of Workers", in *Comparative Labour Law and Industrial Relations*, edited by Blanpain, 1982, pp. 320 ff.

BAMBER G.J., LANSBURY R.D., "Industrial Relations and Technological Change: Towards a Comparative Technology?", International Industrial Relations Association, Vienna, September 1984.

BELLIER Gilles, "Après l'échec des négociations sur la flexibilité", *Droit Social*, February 1985, p. 79.

BERAUD Jean-Marc, *La suspension du contrat de travail*, éditions Sirey, 1980.

BAROIN D., LOOS J., "Protection juridique et couverture sociale du travail à temps partiel en Europe", *Droit Social*, 1982, p. 560.

BLANC-JOUVAN, *Les développements récents de la négociation collective*, (duplicated), Paris, 1986.

BLANPAIN R., (Editor), *Temporary Work and the Law*, Deventer, 1978.

BLANPAIN R., "Ajustements structurels et relations professionnelles: aspects de droit du travail", *Travail et société*, May 1985, pp. 197 and 206.

BOUBLI G., "A propos de la flexibilité de l'emploi: vers la fin du droit du travail", *Droit Social*, 1985, pp. 239-240.

BOYER Robert (ed.), *La flexibilité du travail en Europe*, La Découverte, Paris, 1986.

CARINCI Franco, "New Forms and Aspects of Atypical Employment Relationships: Italy", Report to the Caracas conference, September 1985.

COLLOQUIUM ON INTERNATIONAL LABOUR LAW, *Crise, maintien de l'emploi et partage du travail* (DÄUBLER, VOGEL-POLSKY, OLEA, JAVILLIER, GHERA, NAPIER), Geneva, 1984.

CORDOVA Efrén, "Atypical Employment Relationships", Caracas international conference, September 1985.

CORDOVA Efrén, "De l'emploi total au travail atypique: vers un virage dans l'évolution des relations du travail?", *Revue Internationale du Travail*, vol. 125, no.6, 1986, pp. 715 ff.

DAHRENDORF Ralf, *Classes et conflits de classes dans la société industrielle*, Mouton, Paris, 1972

DAHRENDORF Ralf, "Conflitto e contratto - relazioni industriali e comunità politica in tempo di crisi", *Rivista di diritto del lavoro*, 1978.

DÄUBLER W., FRIANT Martine, "Un récent exemple de flexibilisation législative: la loi allemande pour la promotion de l'emploi du 26 avril 1985", *Droit Social*, September-October 1986, pp. 715 ff.

DÄUBLER Wolfgang, *Das Arbeitsrecht 2*, 2nd edition, Reinbeck, 1981, p. 401.

DAVIES Paul, FREEDLAND Mark, *Labour Law: Texts and Materials*, 2nd edition, Weidenfeld and Nicholson, London, 1984.

DE GRAZIA R., *Le travail clandestin: situation dans les pays industrialisés à économie de marché*, Geneva, ILO, 1983.

DIENAND Christe, "New Forms and Aspects of Atypical Employment Relationships", Dutch report to the Caracas conference, September 1985.

DUPEYROUX Jean-Jacques, *Droit de la Sécurité Sociale*, Editions Dalloz, 1981.

DURÁN LOPEZ Federico, *Modalidades de contratation laboral*, Madrid, 1986, pp. 36 ff.

EWING, "Home Working, a Framework for Reform", *Industrial Law Journal*, no.11, 1982, pp. 94 ff.

FERRARO Giuseppe, "Las nuevas formas de contratacion laboral", in Federico Durán Lopez, *Las relationes laborales y la reorganizacion del sistema productivo*, Cordova, 1983, pp. 91-103.

FALKENBERG Dieter, "Atypische Arbeitsverhältnisse in der Bundesrepublik Deutschland", Caracas conference.

FREEDLAND Mark, "Labour law and Leaflet Law: the Youth Training Scheme of 1983", *Industrial Law Journal*, no.12, 1983, p. 220.

FÜRSTENBERG F., "La réglementation de la dureé du travail en R.F.A.", *Travail et Société*, vol.10, no.2, May 1985, p. 141.

GARCIA MURCIA Joaquim, "El trabajo a tiempo parcial y su regimen juridico en el ordenamiento laboral español", in F. Durán Lopez, *Las relationes laborales y la reorganizacion del sistema productivo*, pp. 141 ff.

GHERA Edoardo, *Diritto del Lavoro*, Caducci editore, Bari, 1985.

GHERA Edoardo, "Crise, maintien de l'emploi et partage du travail", International colloquium, Geneva, 1984.

GIUGNI Gino, "Diritto del lavoro: voce per una enciclopedia", *Giornale di diritto del lavoro e di relazioni industriali*, 1979, no.1.

GIUGNI Gino, "Il diritto del lavoro negli anni '80", *Giornale di diritto del lavoro e di relazioni industriali*, 1982, pp. 373 ff.

HEPPLE Bob, "Security of Employment", Chapter 20 in *Comparative Labour Law*, pp. 355 ff.

HEPPLE Bob, "Restructuring Employment Rights", *Industrial Law Journal*, February 1986, pp. 69-83.

HEPPLE Bob,, NAPIER B., "Temporary Workers and the Law", *Industrial Law Journal*, 1978, pp. 84 ff.

HEPPLE B., O'HIGGINS P., *Employment Law*, 4th edition, Sweet and Maxwell, 1981.

HUTSEBAUT Martin, "Développement des négociations collectives en Europe occidentale 1984 - début 1985", *Revue du travail*, Brussels, 1986, pp. 1 ff.

INSTITUT SYNDICAL EUROPÉEN [European Trade Union Institute], *Flexibilité et emplois: mythes et réalités*, Brussels, 1985.

JALLADE Jean-Pierre, "Mythes et réalités d'une politique du temps partiel", in *Pour une nouvelle politique sociale en Europe* (edited by J. VANDAMME, preface by J. DELORS), Economica, Paris, 1984.

JAVILLIER J.C., "Ordre juridique, relations professionnelles et flexibilité: approches comparatives et internationales", *Droit Social*, January 1986, p. 56.

JEAMMAUD A., LYON-CAEN A. (editors), *Droit du travail, démocratie et crise, en Europe et aux Etats-Unis*, Actes-Sud, Arles, 1986.

KAHN-FREUND O., *Labour and the Law* (Paul Davies and Mark Freedland), 3rd edition, Stevens, 1983.

KESSLER F. ''La réduction de la durée du travail dans la métallurgie allemande et ses conséquences sur les autres branches industrielles'', *Droit Social*, December 1985, p. 850.

KRAVARITOU-MANITAKIS Yota, *L'emploi des femmes en Grèce, en Espagne et au Portugal*, Commission of the European Communities, V12745/83,Fr, 1983.

KRAVARITOU-MANITAKIS Yota, *Evolution des conventions collectives nationales et négociation multinationale dans la CEE: Pour un statut européen*, Institut d'Etudes Européennes, Brussels, 1976.

LEIGHTON Patricia, ''New Forms and Aspects of Atypical Employment Relationships'', English report presented to the Caracas conference, 1985.

LÖWISCH M., ''Das Beschäftigungsforderungsgesetz 1985'', *Betriebs Berater*, 1985.

LYON-CAEN G., LYON-CAEN A., *Droit social international et européen*, 6th edition, Dalloz, 1985.

LYON-CAEN Gérard, ''Plasticité du capital et nouvelles formes d'emploi'', *Droit Social*, no.9-10, 1980, pp. 10 ff.

LYON-CAEN Gérard, ''La bataille truqueé de la flexibilité'', *Droit Social*, December 1985, p. 801.

MITSOU T., ''Concertation et mutations économiques en Grèce au cours des cinq dernières années'', Colloquium on the Mediterranean Countries, Association française d'études des relations professionnelles, Paris, 24-29 April 1986.

MONTEIRO Fernandez Antonio, ''Relaçoes de trabalho atipicas em Portugal'', Caracas international conference, 1985.

MOULY Jean, ''Le social et l'économique: conflit ou convergence'', *Revue Internationale de Travail*, May-June 1986, pp. 385 ff.

NEDO (ATTINSON J., MEAGER Nigel), *Changing Working Patterns: How Companies Achieve Flexibility to Meet New Needs*, London, 1986.

OECHSLIN J.J., ''Travail et flexibilité: le point de vue des employeurs'', *BIS*, February 1985, pp. 203-205.

OLMSTED Barney, ''Un nouveau style de travail fait son apparition:

le partage des emplois'', *Revue Internationale du Travail,* vol.118, May-June 1979.

PELISSIER Jean, ''La relation de travail atypique'', French report presented to the Caracas conference, 1985.

PRADOS DE REYES Francisco Javier, ''Las obligaciones formativas en el contrato de trabajo para la formacion: incidencia en su configuracion juridica'', in Federico Durán Lopez, *Las relaciones laborales,* loc. cit., pp. 115-122.

ROBINSON O., WALLACE J., *Part-time Employment and Sex Discrimination Legislation in Great Britain,* Department of Employment, London, 1984.

RUNGGALDIER U., ''Tendances actuelles du travail italien'', *Droit Social,* December 1985, p. 856.

SANTIAGO Gonzalez Ortega, ''El trabajo temporal de colaboracion social'', in Federico Durn Lopez, loc. cit., pp. 123-129.

SCHNORR G., ''Le travail temporaire: Analyse du droit des Etats-membres des C.E. et propositions relatives à un rapprochement des législations'', *Cahiers de Droit Européen,* 1973, pp. 131 ff.

SOUBIE Raymond, ''Après les négociations sur la flexibilité'', *Droit Social,* 1985, February p. 295, March p. 221, April p. 290.

SPYROPOULOS Georges (editor), *Trade Unions Today and Tomorrow* (two volumes), and the introduction to the first volume; ''Le rôle des syndicats dans un monde en mutation: tendances actuelles et perspectives d'avenir'', in *News,* European Centre for Work and Society (Maastricht, no.11), November 1986.

TSOUKALAS Constantin, ''Classes unidimensionnelles et sujets polyvalents'', *Anti,* 1984, p. 267.

TSOUKALAS C., ''Sujets polyvalents et relations de classes dans le capitalisme contemporain'', *Revue de Sciences Sociales* [Greece], 1985, no.56, p. 3.

VANACHTER O., VRANKEN M., Belgian report to the Caracas conference, 1985.

VENEZIANI Bruno, ''New technology and the contract of employment'', Report to the Jesolo conference, September 1986.

VOGEL-POLSKY Éliane, *Droit Social: Les rapports individuels du travail,* Presses Universitaires de Bruxelles, 1987.

WEDDERBURN William, "The New Industrial Relations Laws in Great Britain", *Labour and Society*, vol.10, January 1985, p. 46.

WEDDERBURN William, *Workers and the Law*, 3rd edition, London, 1986, pp. 116 ff.

ZERDELIS Dimitris, "Le contrat à durée déterminée (droit hellénique)", *Revue de droit du travail* [Greece], vol.45, 1986, pp. 70 and 105.

Studies carried out and published by the Foundation in the field of

NEW FORMS OF WORK AND ACTIVITY

New forms of work and activity: Documentation from a Colloquium; Brussels, April 25, 1986 (1986)
> Unilingual edition
> ISBN 92-825-6712-5   Cat No. SY-48-86-084-EN-C
> Also published in DE/FR/ES
>
> Multilingual edition (EN/DE/FR)
> ISBN 92-825-6418-5   Cat No. SY-46-86-775-3A-C

Legal and contractual limitations to working time in the European Community Member States
> By Prof. Roger Blanpain, University of Leuvin
> Co-Publishers: Kluwer, Law and Taxation Publishers
>   (Deventer, Netherlands).
> ISBN 92-825-6766-4   Cat No. SY-50-87-283-EN-C
> Published only in EN

News Forms of Work — labour law and social security aspects in the European Community
> Prepared for the Foundation by
> Prof. Yota Kravaritou-Manitakis
> ISBN 92-825-7914-X   Cat No. SY-52-88-324-EN-C
> Published only in EN, working paper available in FR on request

167